Oldest on the Bus are a married couple,
both in our mid-fifties now and have alv
years we have got more adventurous in
What started as city breaks around Euro
India whilst on holiday in Goa. These are our recollections of trips we
have made in India; huge thanks must go to Valerie of Valerie Travels
who has enabled us to create such fantastic memories. Over the years
our confidence and trust grew, culminating with a self-arranged trip to
Varanasi. India truly is a magnificent country, explore as much as you can
– there is so much to see.

The Oldest on the Bus name came from our travels around Thailand,
Cambodia and Vietnam, where it was a running joke that we were always
the oldest, surrounded by young backpackers almost half our age. We
even created a blog for our second visit and subsequent travels around
Nepal, Malaysia and Borneo, that can be viewed at the following
address...

https://oldestonthebus.home.blog/

Ironically there is not much bus activity in these India stories; and, in a
further twist, we are a long way from being the oldest ...

Also in the Middle-Aged Travel Adventures series...

Backpacking: Not Just for the Young! Thailand : Cambodia : Vietnam : India

Our Travels Around India

Oldest on the Bus

Foreword

For our first book we had handwritten diaries of our travels around Thailand, Cambodia and Vietnam that culminated with a relaxing two months stay in Goa to unwind and put our feet up. After living out of suitcases for the previous nine weeks it was just what we needed – sunshine, great food and a familiarity of somewhere we have visited so many times in the previous eight years. At the time we had never considered writing the diaries up and getting them published, they were more for our own recollections and memories. A combination of lockdown boredom and my Auntie Doreen (who has always had a massive love of travel), suggesting that they would be an interesting read to others, people who share that same sense of exploration and discovery.

With having nothing written down to look back upon for this book, Our Travels Around India is solely from memories prompted by a vast photo collection, and for two or three trips we also have DVD footage from an old camcorder. The odd review that we posted on TripAdvisor has also come in useful, giving an indication of our thoughts at the time. How does our retrospection now, a few years further on compare to our thinking back then? Some recollections and feelings were so fresh in our heads that it felt like we were there just yesterday - who could ever forget their first experience of India? Others were stored somewhere far deeper, dislodged and only recalled by looking not just through the albums but also the external hard drives of photographs that had never made the cut! A trip to India though is not as one dimensional as sight alone. It is an assault on all your senses, the sounds of the constantly parping horns from the traffic, shouts of 'taxi?' as you walk by a card-playing driver and the honk or bell of the bread man selling his bakes. The smells, both good and bad, the rotting rubbish somewhere near the bottom of the spectrum and the aroma of fantastic food most definitely at the top. Spices, and the smells coming from the restaurants suitably bring us on to taste. For lovers of Indian cuisine, you are immediately transported to food heaven, if spicy curries are not your bag, then the apple pie and ice cream from Infantaria is equally divine. Working our way through all the senses, the touch must be that of the sand between your toes as you walk carefree along the beach... far better than the gritty feeling it has once it is in your bed when you wake up next morning, having trailed it there from the dusty roads the night before!

Over the course of this book, we look all the way back to our first visit in 2008, a one-week trip as that was all the holiday we had left from our annual allowance, right through to our final two visits (for now) that were both in 2016. The first of the two in 2016 was a two month stay, part of our Asian travel adventure, the second being the more traditional two-week booking. We had intentionally taken a break from visiting at that point, not because we had fallen out of love with the country but because we had visited all the places that were at the top of our 'tick list.' Our intended return in 2021 was subsequently ruined by Covid, but it is just a matter of time before we spend another winter there, or at least a couple of months - and hopefully we can finally get to visit Shimla! Whilst our number of visits does not compare to some who travel to Goa year after year for some winter sun, we have put our time to good use and have been fortunate enough to have explored our way around many of the incredible highlights this vast country has to offer.

What initially attracted us to the country was the food, neither of us can get enough of it, be that the afternoon snacks of samosas, batata wadas or the endless curry dish options in the evening! So, for us a holiday where you can indulge in your favourite meals is perfect. It might seem strange to many but we are not beach people; we both love the idea of relaxing on a sunbed for hours on end, just reading or people watching, but the reality is that after two or three days of that we are bored and restless. The evenings we love, start the night off with some fantastic tasty food and follow that up visiting some great local bars serving ice cold beer and local spirits - ideal for just watching the world go by. Our biggest problem was how do we fill our days? For us, (and appreciate many may not agree), it is a long way to travel just to lay on a beach – especially when there are such incredible places a short internal flight (or train journey) away. We concluded that to enjoy the best of both worlds we would book a fortnights holiday to Goa, but then also have a 'plan,' something away from the coast for a few days that would also be a tick on the bucket list. A little bit of beach, exploration of somewhere new for a few days, and then back for more beach or pool to unwind seems to work well for us.

Across the years we have visited the Golden Triangle, taking in Delhi, Agra and Jaipur. We loved Jaipur so much that we subsequently made a second visit to Rajasthan and explored Jodhpur and Udaipur, an incredibly beautiful city that was quite serene and a pleasure to wander around. Changes to our return connecting flight in Mumbai meant that we had to tag on an additional day there! From Goa a single but long train journey into Karnataka to visit Hampi gave us another memorable few days away in a place we had never even heard of! Kerala was a tour and beach stay; a rice boat on the backwaters of Alleppey and the city of Cochin before heading to the hills to visit the tea plantations. We got to experience a home stay before moving on to visit Periyar National Park. From the beach resort of Kovalum we arranged ourselves a trip down to the Southernmost tip of India, Kanyakumari.

The same year we also visited the other end of the country, Amritsar! What a place this is, most famous as the home of the Sikh pilgrimage site of the Golden Temple but also a place of shame from our colonial past, the massacre at Jallianwala Bagh. Close to Amritsar is the most joyous place we have ever visited in India; the Wagah border ceremony is a must see. Every night is party night at this crazy border closing ceremony as Pakistan and Indian soldiers try to outdo each other in moustaches, high kicking marches and posturing – all in front of dancing, chanting high-energy crowds. Mysore and its stunning palace (via a one-night stay in Bangalore), was our destination to break up our stay another year. In 2016 we finally made our way to Varanasi, it had always been a tricky one to reach due to flight connection times, but in our two months stay we had no excuses not to make it. It more than lived up to expectations, a truly fascinating place.

There is one lady who deserves a special mention for the trips and adventures that India has given us, many of you who have visited Calangute will know her already. Valerie Rodrigues of Valerie Travels has become a good friend over the years, and we have been fortunate enough to visit her home and experience her cooking (it is delicious). Even better than that, when we rented an apartment by her shop, she was kind enough to come round and give us some Indian cooking lessons! For anyone who is looking for excursions, whether that is a day trip or a few nights further away in other parts of India then we can highly recommend Valerie.

For us travel is not just about the sights you get to see upon arriving at your destination, it is about enveloping yourself in the whole experience - the getting there is just as much part of the memory as the carefully taken photographs that you take once you have arrived. There are so many proverbs about life and journeys, some funny, others profound; but the general rule of thumb is that wherever you are heading be sure to enjoy the getting there.

Travel programs on TV are always popular, usually presented by a celebrity who spends time between filming in plush hotels, eating in the finest restaurants and being chauffeured around in luxury. For most of us travel is a very different experience altogether; budget hotels rather than five-star, street food ahead of swanky restaurants, - but we still get to see the same star attraction at the end, be that the Taj Mahal, Golden Temple or the ghats of Varanasi. What we would argue though, is that it is the budget traveller who has the more fulfilling experience, the unintentional comedy moments, the better food and we also get to meet some fantastic characters along the way - who you remember long after your return home. It is not all win though, the celebrity presenter no doubt sleeps in the comfier bed, dries themselves on softer, bigger towels and even has reliable electricity – but personally we still wouldn't want to swap our travels for theirs.

Across the book there should be stories that anyone who has visited India can relate to, from the humming, meditating hotelier to the service station incident on route between Jaipur and Delhi. Of course, travel is all about the places you visit, and whilst we have added some basic information or background in parts, hopefully it is on the 'light' side rather than anything too heavy. We didn't want to list facts and figures like a guidebook, but more a brief background or insight and then convey them in our own words and feelings, was it how we imagined it to be and where disappointed, or at least never lived up to our expectations. Hopefully the stories we tell may jog your own memories, and have you searching through your own photo albums – after all what is the point of travelling if it is not to reminisce and remember those magical moments?

Index

April 2008 - Goa Virgins

Christmas 2007 and we both have a few days off work, and with holiday adverts on television in full flow we decide to make some plans of our own. We both work for the same company, so our holiday year and annual entitlements are the same, we both have five days that need to be used up by the end of April. The Canaries don't really excite, we have done them before, so if we want some winter sun then we need to look further afield.

Goa had always been on the radar, we both love curry as our local Indian restaurant can vouch for, there is not many Friday evenings that we aren't in The Star of India for their banquet meal! Sri Lanka had been our honeymoon destination a couple of years previous so we knew what to expect – hot, humid, hectic, roaming cows and crazy tuk-tuks. On the Thomson website (many years before the rebrand to TUI) we find a week's holiday; the flights are from Birmingham and the price is pretty good. A little bit more research, a chat with a guy from work who was a regular visitor to Goa and then a trip to the Cooperative Travel Agent and we were booked. A seven-night stay at the Aldeio Bello in Calangute. We are reliably informed that Calangute is a great resort, nestled nicely in-between the busier Baga and the quieter more relaxed Candolim. Bring on March, I know it is wishing your time away but who really enjoys the dark cold months of January and February in the UK?

By the beginning of February we are crossing the days off, there is nothing like a countdown to a holiday! We fill in the visa applications, attach the photographs and send off our passports, not forgetting to include the return pre-paid tracked envelope for their return. Fortunately, we both work in office based administrative roles so the visa application forms did not really phase us, but more left us puzzled of why they needed so much information! We are just travelling for a week's holiday, we want to spend some money in your country, why make life so difficult? With those sent off it was just a short wait before they were successfully returned to us, visa stuck nicely inside and that was it, we are all set to go.

Back in 2008 neither of us were on Facebook, nowadays we would join a travel group relevant to our destination and be able to find so much information on there from some knowledgeable and helpful posters, that option wasn't available to us. Our sole source of tips, advice and recommendations was from TripAdvisor. Worryingly when we checked the latest reviews on the Aldeio Bello the advice was unanimously 'Don't Stay

Here.' If it had been just the one post then that would not have bothered us at all, unfortunately it was every post-dated within the last month! All the reviews that we had previously read were now gone, instead TripAdvisor only had these...

Please Read prior to booking ....

... the outside has not seen a coat of paint since it was built ... and looks like a prisoner of war camp... furniture which should be put in a skip... the bed was a wooden frame with hardboard base and the mattress, if you can call it that, was thinner than the cushions I have on my bench in the garden... I felt I had to write this review as I really didn't want anyone to book this hotel without knowing how bad it really is...

- - - - -

Aldeio Bello -Read before booking - be warned - A honest report.

The hotel itself was visibly dirty, the hotel grounds were dirty, the table cloths were dirty, the whole surrounding area was dirty, when eating we spent most of the time chasing flies from the table and food... The hotel is adjacent to a homeless people's shanty site and the noises from there early morning were most annoying making sleep impossible, all and sundry have a right of way through the hotel grounds at any time.

- - - - -

All the tour operators need to re-asses this one!

The photo's you see on holiday companies' website are very cleverly taken, looking at the pool, building on your right they don't tell you there's a shanty town to the left. You know it's there as a cockerel who cannot tell the time will crow from 1am-6am.The women doing their laundry & slapping down wet clothes on rocks will wake you at 5am, the bread seller will wake you at 6am by ringing his bell...A land owner right of way dispute between the hotel & shanty town means as you have meals/drinks, trucks, vans, tuk-tuk's & herds of cows will walk through the hotel!
Our room when I walked in, I cried! As you walked in a window on your

left didn't have glass but ornate concrete work letting bugs etc crawl straight in, ripped sofa & chairs, rusty fridge, no tv, table covered in fag burns! Very hard single beds with dirty covers on & sweat smelling pillows, also stained. A fan that we thought would fly off the wall & air con that sounded like a cow giving birth! All rooms have another room like a utility room, with 2 poles going from wall to wall, no coat hangers but you could hang your towels over. No wardrobes. Shower room with broken soap dish, cracked mirror. Water spurts from shower head & we had to put a flannel over it so water didn't hit the electrical water tank above!

- - - - -

Read this before booking!!!

The room was dirty, the shower rusty and bare wires were hanging from the air conditioning unit which was so loud I am surprised the windows didn't shake. Our bathroom was in a worst state than some of the public toilets (I know the brochure said the place was basic but I at least expected it to be clean). The brochure also said the hotel was in a quiet setting next to a local traditional village. Actually, it was so noisy that it was impossible to sleep at night. There was a cockerel which crowed throughout the night and the place was surrounded by dogs which barked and fought all night. Women washing clothes early in the morning was too noisy to let anyone sleep and the tenants of these huts spat and urinated in front of you.

PLEASE BE AWARE THAT HOLIDAY COMPANIES AND BROCHURES ARE MISLEADING AS FAR AS THIS HOLTEL IS CONCERNED!

Something had changed drastically between us booking in the first week of January and the end of February, we were that concerned that we popped back into the travel agents to see if there was anything we could do regarding our booking. The answer was yes, but the costs involved were about the same as what we had paid for our holiday, oh well let us prepare for the worst whilst nervously hoping for the best.

Its over fourteen years ago since we flew out, so we don't remember a lot about the flight itself, it may have been around midnight when we landed but the heat was still like the opening of the oven door as we climbed down the steps and made our way from the plane to the terminal building. The chaos of the arrival hall is still a recollection, or more of a mental scar; something that we always came to dread on arriving in Goa. Perhaps it's the combination of tiredness, heat and queues, the form filling and immigration that makes it such a nightmare start to the holiday. And that is even before you even get to baggage reclaim...

With immigration / passport control done, it was time to collect our luggage. It was no surprise after the length of time it had taken to pass through passport control that the cases had already been offloaded into neat rows with just a handful still going round on the carousel - it had taken an age for a plane load of visitors to have their visas stamped. We had been pre-warned about this bit, once you get your hands on your case keep a very tight grip, a firm no to the grabbing hands of the porters who are just aching to carry them that short journey for a tip. Informed of our bus number by the travel rep we fend off the porters and make our way to the coach.

The coach was an experience, with the boot already full our luggage was put on the roof – the first time we had ever experienced that. Inside was also, shall we say different? Fans attached to the framework between the windows were just like the fans from our office - unusual, but also essential – it was roasting. The 'No Spitting Signs' - I don't think I know of anyone who would even consider spitting on a bus in the first place, but then again, we have never visited India before. The seats were worn, the bus was old and unlike any we had been on before - while we were taking in our surroundings the last passengers boarded along with the Thomson rep...

It was one of the best welcome speeches that we have had on an arrival anywhere. Humorous, but as we would discover over the next few days also very apt. Such gems about the dangers of swimming in the sea, do not be reassured by the sight of lifeguards, more than likely they cannot even swim. Warnings about traffic, cows and elephants, and a reminder that all the usual rules you know need forgetting, there are no highway code rules here, or if there are they are generally ignored. Advice about the comfort of your bed and pillows – if your pillow is too hard there is not much point in asking for a second, that would be like resting your head on two bricks rather than just the one. Fortunately, we do like a firm bed...

In no time we were approaching the resorts, a group were dropped off near the Red Lion pub and the rep walked them down a dark alley somewhere in that area. There were a few people wandering the streets but nearly everything was closed for the night, tarpaulins over the front of some of the stalls by the roundabout that we would later discover takes you down to the beach. With the rep back on board we headed down what we now know to be the Calangute to Baga road, and before long the bus turned right down what was little more than a single-track road. One more right and then we were there, the Aldeio Bello. On first impressions it looked just the job. The pool was gently lapping in the moonlight, a building labelled up as 'The Pub' and a good-sized seating area where meals would be served.

We were shown to our room, informed what time breakfast would be served and we were also handed some meal vouchers. Although we were booked in on bed and breakfast basis, as part of our deal we had three evening meals included at the on-site restaurant. Our room was basic, and that is being generous; the wardrobe was more like a tall kitchen unit, and along with the bed, that was the limit to the furniture in that room. The second room had a portable television perched on the fridge and one chair, the solitary chair was so threadbare and worn that when you sat on it your bottom was skimming the floor. Getting back out of it was near on impossible. The room was immaculately clean though, so considering some of the shocking reviews we were more than happy – after all who travels all that way to sit inside your accommodation?

After a reasonable night's sleep, we were awoken by barking dogs, one of the many complaints that people had written about on TripAdvisor. If it hadn't been the dogs that had woken us it would have been the cockerel anyway! It was different, but in a good way, the smiling staff were already making up for any minor issues in the quality of the furnishings! Breakfast was perfect for anyone who was indecisive, the only decisions to make were tea or coffee and how you would like your eggs. Fried egg, scrambled egg or no egg on your toast was as difficult as the food related question could get.

Having been fed we set off to explore, heading up towards Baga first. We had heard all about Tito's Lane and thought we would go look in daylight, so we knew exactly where it was come the darkness this evening. Having found that, we continued onto the beach and turned left back towards Calangute, and with the sun beating down upon us, the time having gone past 11 a.m. - why not sit at a shack and enjoy our first beers of the holiday? We must have been obvious targets to the highly trained Goan pedlars; fresh off the plane, its March so very pale from an English winter - in no time the beach sellers were gathering around us. Scarf lady and massage lady were easily fobbed off, but a guy selling a carved stone was not going to be palmed off as easily, he was persistent.

We were so close to being ripped off on our first ever day in Goa. Arriving in the middle of the night and having wandered around without going into any shops we were just the kind of customers he was looking for. I am sure you have all seen the stones carved with one elephant inside another, a latticed stomach through which you can see another elephant inside? It was one of those. He gave a great story of how he sourced the stones; they were a long way from home and he had to walk miles each day to find them. They had to be just perfect, not too big, not too small, the right kind of shine and marbling. He would then carry these stones all the way back home to where his blind Uncle would hand carve these unique sculptures by touch alone. He was bringing them out of his bag as if they were priceless, each was lovingly wrapped in an old rag, he would dust them off and caress them gently before passing them over to us. Not just elephants, his uncle had done crocodiles too from stones that were long and thin rather than round...

To be fair we were impressed, we had certainly never seen anything like them, but then again at this stage we hadn't visited the fixed price shops by Redondo's where the shelves were full of these 'unique' pieces. I cannot remember what price he was asking for, and I cannot remember either how we avoided buying one! I just assume he wanted so much for it (we had taken in his story hook, line and sinker), that we would not have wanted to insult him with a counter offer that he would most likely have snapped our hands off for anyway - whilst putting a hard done by look on his face at the same time!

Our first ever meal in Goa, and to this day it is still the first place we eat every time we visit, was at Mirabai's. Fourteen years on and it is still the best curry I have ever eaten! It was their Chilli Chicken dish, spicy and with three dried chillies sticking out the top of the bowl. Over the course of the week, we must have visited there another four times, when you are in India for seven days only, we felt it necessary to have a full meal at both lunch time and in the evening! As I said, as part of our Goa tradition we always have our first meal at Mirabai's, but that dish has never been as good as it was in March 2008. Over the years maybe the chef has changed, year on year the recipe has certainly been altered. One year the chicken was in batter (it was not nice at all), but still it doesn't put us off, just hoping and still remembering how good our first ever meal in India was!

From Mirabai's we headed on towards the beach and then turned left towards Candolim. At this time there was still a beached oil tanker just off the coast, reading up on it, it had run aground during a storm in the year 2000 and was stuck on that sandbank for the next twelve years! We are not talking far out to sea either, thirty or forty metres off shore. The Rovers Return gave us an opportunity for a bit of shade, a chance to put our feet up and enjoy another beer, or two. When we were looking to head back to our hotel we got lost, walking along the beach we just could not find where we needed to turn off – with hindsight we should have made a mental note of which shack the sandy path was by! In the end we walked all the way up to Baga, down Tito's Lane and back along the main road, that is one way to work up an appetite.

With looking to cram as much into our short stay as possible we booked ourselves onto the Crocodile and Bird Watching tour as well as the Spice Plantations and Temples tour. We cannot remember what agent we used but it was down by the Mira Hotel (which had a fantastic Thai restaurant attached to it in those days).

For the Crocodile Tour it was a short bus journey before we arrived at the river side where we boarded a boat ran by 'Jake the Snake.' A brief but funny introduction was the prelude to a great trip, and for all Jakes joking around he really knew his stuff, highly informative about not just the crocodiles but also the bird life that was far more abundant than the crocs! To this day we still use some of his phrases, as he would be pointing birds out - he would shout, 'sitting bird, sitting bird' if it were resting in a tree, or a 'flying bird, flying bird' if it was up in the sky. Considering that he must do the same trip day after day his enthusiasm was infectious.

We did eventually see a couple of crocodiles; one was right up on the bank and fast asleep, so the boat was able to be turned right round so that everyone could get a good look and take some snaps (very apt description for photographing a crocodile!). This must be a prime place to find these huge creatures, with them being cold blooded they spend a lot of time in the sun, bathing their selves on the mudbanks of the Cumbarjua canal. Jake informs us that these mugger crocodiles are less dangerous than salt water crocs, but no one was too keen on putting that theory to the test. The way he described them made them sound very lazy, living on a diet of sick fish, crabs, cats and dogs. Larger crocodiles would easily be able to tackle a small deer or buffalo, but it sounded like they were only interested in food that was passing close by! The second one was right by the water edge, hiding in the shadows of an overhanging tree. It was difficult to pick out initially, so good was its camouflage, and with that the boat had unsettled it and it took to the water. The trip along the mangroves was good fun, not something you can get to do in many places and with it being just a half day excursion we would be back in Calangute for lunch!

A few interesting 'mugger' crocodile facts...

They are known to eat rocks as ballast, it helps enable them to stay under water for up to an hour at a time.

From a clutch of around thirty eggs only two or three hatchlings are expected to survive, the remainder succumb to rats, mongoose, birds and of course humans...

Four metres is as large as they grow up to, that's just over thirteen feet!

To communicate they bark like a dog, not sure if that is a yap of a Jack Russell or something larger and more aggressive though...

With it being March, we were fortunate enough to be there for the Holi festival, or Festival of Colour as it is also known. This added even more vibrancy to the temples part of the spice gardens tour. It was another mini-bus journey to Ponda; the spice gardens were reached by crossing a long bamboo bridge where your guide would then welcome you with a coconut drink before taking you on a guided tour pointing out all the different spices. It was interesting to learn more about your spices (and nuts), how they were grown and which part of the plant they were. The downside was that you always knew the hard sell would be coming at some point! With the gardens part over it was into the showroom where you were handed leaflets with listings of all the ailments that could be cured if you purchased their spice blends.

Away from the spices there was the opportunity to bathe an elephant, or at least scrub its back with a coconut shell. The water looked a little grim to say the least and we both turned that option down, not wanting to look like we had wallowed in mud for the remainder of the day! More up our street, or at least we thought it was, the opportunity to try the local tipple, Feni. Brewed from either the cashew apple, (which is the fruit just above where the cashew nut hangs) or coconut. We found them both equally horrible. The first step in making Feni is the crushing of cashew apples (or coconut) until the juice runs out into an earthen or copper pot which is buried deep under the ground for fermentation. Following fermentation, the juice is distilled three times by boiling on a woodfire producing a fiery clear drink that is around 45% proof. For many years I always thought the best place for Feni would for it to have been left in that pot underground, never to be dug up – then one year someone convinced me to give it a second chance, but as a long drink. That was me converted, add Sprite to Feni as a mixer and it is delicious.

The Temple complex was the Shree Mangesh Temple, close to Panaji the capital of Goa. It is a Hindu temple dating back to the sixteenth century, and is one of the most frequently visited in Goa. It was attractive enough already, but with-it being Holi the outside of the temple had trestles covered with bowls of all different coloured powders, no doubt in readiness for the festival of colour that would kick off later in the day. For keen photographers it was a sea of colour, add to that all the local ladies in their best outfits it was the perfect time to be visiting. The architecture is a mix of domes and balustrades, all looking pristine, but the highlight for us was the seven-storey lamp tower, not a pagoda, but remarkably similar in style. With our culture done for the day it was time to board the mini-bus for our journey back to Calangute.

We were enjoying our stay at the Aldeio Bello, what some of the reviews said were true, the furniture was shocking, but hey, we had not paid the price of a stay in a five-star hotel. Whilst the towels may have been threadbare, or even holy in some cases they were always replaced each day and appeared to be clean. The room was swept on a regular basis and we were enjoying the pool, chatting and having a drink with the other guests. The village behind the hotel was interesting to us, yes wash day was noisy with the slapping of clothes on a rock but we were fascinated rather than annoyed by daily life over the other side of the fence. The ladies, as usual in Asia seemed to be doing all the work, using their heads to carry things upon seemed to be the norm. Early evening and the cows would wander by the pub, and with it being our first ever visit we just had to take photos, isn't travel all about experiencing different ways of life?

On the dusty track from the hotel to the main Calangute – Baga road the streetlights were the sort of strip lighting you only see in kitchens or office blocks back home; I was amazed that they worked at all just hung dangling like that. Sandy coloured dogs slept in the shade, but none of them ever seemed interested in us. Being a backroad, it also seemed to be an unofficial men's urinal, on a handful of occasions we see locals having a pee, but I guess that is a consequence of having no public toilets? It did not take us long to discover why there was that 'No Spitting' sign on the bus! Unfortunately, it is not just the spitting, the whole noisy clearing of the throat beforehand was often the pre-cursor to the spit itself. Just as you meet the main road there was a little bar, Toff Toffs; that became a regular haunt of ours – both on the way out each evening and as our last port of call heading home.

Looking through the photographs gives us a clue as to where we were eating and drinking, The Cricketers was a regular stop, that would have been on route to Mirabai's for food and there was a sports bar we visited on a few occasions on the main road, I believe that was called Eclipse? It was a very popular place with the British tourists and had a quiz night for definite as we entered it and only went and won! Oddly I only remember one question, something along the lines of what fruit is in a tarte tatin, we knew the answer (apples) as we had seen one cooked on Master Chef just a week or two earlier! The table next to us advised us to take the bottle of spirits as the prize, rather than a round of drinks; and that started our love affair with the local Honey Bee brandy. The Log Cabin is the only other pub we remember visiting, there was a very funny Indian comedian slash singer on the night we were there. All that way from home and next door to the bar, or very close at least, was a fish and chip shop!

Food wise we ate upstairs in Infantaria, where there would often be a live singer. Pork Sorpotel was on the menu and with that being another dish that I had never seen on a menu back home I had to give it a try. It is best described as a Goan sausage, very tasty but a little on the dry side for my liking. I think the attraction of Infantaria was that it would always have a beer deal on the blackboard for if you were ordering food, perhaps three bottles of Kingfisher for a bargain price to wash your food down with. We had discovered here one afternoon when we popped in for egg chop and samosas, we then caught sight of their cake selection and discovered their apple pie... Big chunks of apple with a sprinkling of cinnamon under a golden pastry, it is making me hungry now just writing it.

The Thai restaurant by the Mira Hotel had been recommended to us, it was a little bit more expensive than our usual meal but the setting was very nice, decorative lights hanging from the trees and the tables being elegantly (for Goa) presented. The food was delicious and it did have that 'special' feeling that merited the extra expense, no doubt still an absolute bargain to what you would pay back home! A few years later we would be staying at the Mira, but by then the Thai restaurant had been relocated further down the road. From memory it was a German guy who owned the place along with his Thai wife, they certainly were one of the most popular restaurants in Calangute at that time as booking was essential.

The only other place we can remember by name is The Tibetan Kitchen, from the roundabout heading towards the beach it was on the left-hand side. All you can see from the road itself is a small sign directing you down the dark alley alongside a shop, the alley is short with a big step at some point before it opens out to the restaurant which is lovely. It is one of those places that exceeds your expectations on arrival, in fact, over the years we have never missed a visit. It is famous for its Mo Mo's, (we ate a lot of them in Nepal one year), and be sure to have the soup too (it even used to say that on the menu!). We later discovered that they also do a fantastic steak with crushed garlic potatoes and a well-presented salad, often our go to meal when we are either curried out or have a flight next day!

There were other places that we ate at, but they obviously did not leave much of an impression! We ate our three meals at the hotel, so the food there must have been good, and the menu must have been more expansive than what it offered for breakfast. It is safe to say that if the first meal had been a let-down there is no way we would have eaten there again, especially when such delicious food was available right on the doorstep!

Before we knew it our time was up, we experienced a wash out on our final day, it poured and poured for hours on end. In some ways that made our departure a little easier? One thing for certain is that we knew we would be returning, and not just for a week... So, after all the one-star reviews on TripAdvisor we bucked the trend and gave it a solid three out of five. All these years on we don't remember having any power cuts, though I am guessing we had at least one as in the review we left it does get a mention...

Pleasant stay despite worrying reviews

After reading the reviews for this hotel we were concerned enough to see about changing our accommodation, but as it was near to departure date the costs were high.

A lot of what is in other reviews was true, the rooms are very basic, beds are hard & it is next to a local village who have access through the hotel grounds (literally in front of the bar area so no interference to guests at all). Another review complains about flies, presumably posher hotels don't have them?!?

Reaching the hotel is down a small road, but not as far as some people would have you believe, 2 to 3 minutes at the most. There were dogs but they tended to be asleep & never approached us in all the times we were up & down the road. The road is badly lit so would recommend packing a torch for after dark, also handy when the hotel loses its power supply (although they do provide candles in your room).

The rooms, as already mentioned were very basic, but they were cleaned on a daily basis. Hotel staff were all very friendly & the food at the restaurant was excellent. Breakfast was eggs, eggs or eggs.

Wouldn't hesitate to go back & although accommodation was basic you felt you really were experiencing local life with the village next door rather than being in some faceless 5-star complex where you could have been anywhere in the world.

November 2010 - Goa and the Golden Triangle

There was no visit for us in 2009; I, Wayne, had been celebrating my fortieth birthday with a family holiday taking in a safari. With the departure for Kenya late March and running into April we had to take some of that holiday out of each year's entitlement. No doubt that had left us short on the money side too, but it was worth every penny. We have done safaris since in both Sri Lanka and South Africa, both amazing experiences – but we have still never seen a leopard! On the plus side we had bought a camcorder so I have been able to watch footage from that, as well as trawl through the photo albums before writing this.

November 2010, and Calangute was again our destination in North Goa; having loved our first stay there we had no reason to change resort. The Aldeio Bello had disappeared from the brochures, so a new hotel was a must. With more options of travel companies in those days, we eventually booked with Jewel in the Crown who predominantly sold holidays in Goa and trip add-ons. A bit like TUI these days, any excursion you book through them is top dollar, so we looked to source our own tour of the Golden Triangle. With recommendations sourced through TripAdvisor we soon had a five-day trip taking in Delhi, Agra and Jaipur arranged for a few days after our arrival.

The flight to Goa was horrendous, we had never flown with Monarch before (and we never did again). Talk about there being lack of leg room in the cabin, we had never felt so crammed in, and neither of us are taller than five foot eight! If that was not bad enough, how do you like frozen chicken for your flight meal? As well as food poisoning you could have broken your teeth on it, there was still a chunk of ice attached! Needless to say, that put us both off our food... The airport experience and bus journey were just the same as we remembered, only this time we were better prepared for it.

We were staying at the Senhor Angelo on this occasion, so for those of you who know Calangute that is on the beach side of the Calangute to Baga road; past the Cricketers Pub, follow the road round to the left at Mirabai's, then round to the right and there it is. Of all the Goa hotels we have stayed in over the years, this is our favourite. The rooms were still basic, but once again they were kept clean. There was a lovely relaxed atmosphere around the place, perhaps because it was such a small hotel. The breakfast options were just the same as we had before, but with the extra option of jam.

The pool area was very nice, and some of the comfiest sunbeds we have experienced anywhere – nothing flash or expensive about them, but more being made of lots of large elastic bands that meant you sank into them perfectly and could sit or lay without going numb within the hour. Best of all the pool area had a little bar that even offered credit, you were just asked to settle your bill every other day rather than running up a big tab. What was also unusual was the age of the guests, some of them were younger than us! Each evening there would be a group of us who would meet up for drinks at the pool bar before all heading our separate ways for evening meals, there was a nice feel about the place.

If we hadn't remembered having power cuts at the Aldeio Bello, we do from our stay at the Senhor Angelo. Every evening around the same time the power would go without fail; probably caused by us all trying to shower at the same time to meet up at the bar. There was one Scottish guy who was very funny; a big chap who was convinced he was wearing his tiny wife's underwear, blaming his uncomfortable situation on having to root around the suitcase and getting dressed in the dark...

We only had a few days in resort before we were flying onto Delhi for our tour, but in those few days we made a couple more discoveries that have improved and enhanced our visits to Goa ever since. Firstly, we discovered Valerie of Valerie Travels fame. Her shop was on the main road close to the top of our turning, so we initially used to pop in just for currency exchange. We got talking about trips and discovered all the services she offered, not only the local excursions but to further flung parts of India as well. From that visit onwards we have always used Valerie for every trip we have done, we book our internal flights ourselves, months in advance as you get better prices by booking early, and then Valerie sorts out our accommodation and drivers, entry fees etc. The lady is amazing, a proper force of nature, and she tailors each booking to exactly what you are looking for.

Our other 'discovery' was Madhu's, the best bar we have found anywhere. It is in an excellent location for people watching, it serves ice cold beer, a selection of spirits and even has an ice bucket on occasions! The prices are rock bottom and you even get a friendly dog to stroke thrown in; there is nothing fancy though, simple plastic chairs, a dusty floor, but more importantly no 'entertainment.' It is a great place to just share a table and chat to people without the disturbance of bingo or karaoke. When you are ready for another drink just hold up your empty and a replacement is swiftly delivered to your table! At the end of the evening, you settle your bill - it was never more than five pounds for the two of us, but that was enough to have us staggering off home...

After two or three lazy days split between the pool and the beach it was time for our flight to Delhi. Luckily, internal flights within India run far more smoothly than international ones, it was a relative breeze passing through the airport in Goa. I guess what does help is that internal flights seem to run in daytime hours, rather than departing (or arriving), in the dead of the night. We were still a little apprehensive though as we had booked this ourselves, albeit through a recommended company online - what if we arrived in Delhi and there was no one at the airport to collect us? Our arrival in Delhi was as effortless as our departure, and much to our relief there was a guy holding our names up waiting for our arrival. He spoke excellent English and handed us a very professional looking itinerary; contact numbers for if we had any issues, times of pick up, our hotels, places we would be taken to see, (but not go in), and places that we would visit with our tickets included. He explained to us that we would have the same driver for the entire five days but we would have a different guide in each city, so far so good. We were introduced to our driver who spoke very few words of English, hopefully enough for us to get by. And then the guy who was fluent left us, he had someone else to collect...

It was dusk in Delhi, but so much darker due to all the smog – we had noticed it as we had come into land but thought it might just have been local to the airport, the fumes from the planes. Our hotel was a drab looking building from the outside, but once you were inside it was pleasant enough, more functional than memorable. We collected the keys for our room and took our bags up before heading straight back out to explore. It is safe to say we did not venture far, daylight had about gone and it was proper foggy, you could barely see across the road. So much for looking for somewhere to eat, it would have to be at the hotel.

The hotel food was ok, but expensive – or at least compared to what we had been paying in Goa. The restaurant itself was quite a depressing place, down in the bowels of the hotel, no windows – but then with this fog there would have been nothing to see anyway. Maybe it is just us but we are not keen on eating in hotel restaurants, especially when they are virtually empty. The staff were too attentive, watching us like hawks – do we look the type who would steal the cutlery? Our biggest mistake was when they asked us if we would like a beer with our meal, naturally we said yes please. After a long, long wait the waiter returned with two cans of Fosters and we were charged about five pounds for each of them, if only there was a Delhi branch of Madhu's...

Breakfast was a feast, buffet style so it was the perfect opportunity to have Indian food, puri's and parathas, for the first meal of the day as well as the last! As well as the local food options there was also a full English, but with those horrible chicken sausages. The restaurant had far more of an atmosphere in the morning, more hustle and bustle, so we did enjoy our start to the day and made the most of the fruits on offer with plentiful cups of chai.

Our driver arrived in good time; out of habit we are both very punctual – if we are to be somewhere for 9 a.m., we will be there a good ten minutes prior to that, and our driver was of the same ilk, he was always there waiting for us throughout the trip. One of the things that I have never forgotten is that as we were getting in the car there was a guy on the building site next to the hotel who was having a full wash in the street, he simply stood in a large bucket and used the hose pipe to rinse himself down – welcome to Delhi! The traffic was chaos but we were mesmerised by it, it was different to being stuck in a traffic jam back home where you quickly lose the will to live. You are in one of the world's biggest cities, its rush hour, and the traffic is brought to a standstill by someone herding their goats around the traffic island! The fog had dissipated to smog, so still no sign of a blue sky, but it was hot! The buses were still covered in adverts from the Commonwealth games that Delhi had recently hosted, they were also absolutely rammed, people hanging from the doorways on all of them. It is a brave person required to take on the daily commute in this city! As we sit in slow moving traffic the motor cyclists make better progress, using the pavements rather than having the patience to sit and wait.

Before too long we arrive at our first destination, the Jama Masjid (Friday Mosque), one of the largest Mosques in India. Everything is running like clockwork, our guide for the day is already there, and after a quick introduction and him locking his motorbike helmet in the boot of the car we are on our way, Alison has dressed in what we thought was appropriate clothing, the trousers are well below the knee and her shoulders are all covered, the guide gives it the thumbs up and in we go. It is our first experience of the scale of things in India, this place is massive, we are bowled over by it. Not just for size but the decorative carvings and artwork. In the centre of the walled enclosure is a huge pond, or is it for bathing feet? We are not sure, there is lots of shoes abandoned here but it is mainly being used as a giant bird bath, pigeons everywhere! It turns out that our first suspicions were correct, it is in fact an ablution tank, it is there for washing your face, arms, head and feet.

Our guide gives us a brief history of the place, most of which would leave our heads over the next five days, so much information would be bestowed upon us! One thing that we had remembered though was that it was built in the mid seventeenth century by the Mughal Emperor Shah Jahan, that is him of the Taj Mahal fame. Whilst everyone associates him with building such a grand monument to his wife as a great romantic gesture, reality is that he was not a very nice bloke. He was the fifth Mughal Emperor, but before taking that title he had to defeat and kill his own brother. No doubt having done that to immediate family he had no such qualms about executing all other rivals to his throne...

We must have been in there for ten minutes before someone approaches Alison with a bright orange robe to put on, all very friendly and smiling, but she has failed to meet the stringent dress codes! Fully robed up, we can carry on and head up one of the minarets. Now I am not great with heights but do feel comfortable on the way up as its fully enclosed, much like climbing a spiral staircase in a lighthouse. Once we are at the top the views are hampered by the smog, but I was still feeling safe as the railings are neck height. Looking down and you can see the throng of people going about their day; cycle rickshaws, street vendors and shoppers all scurrying around below. The shops look shabby, signs hanging everywhere, tin extensions perched precariously on higher levels, but the streets themselves are very elegant, with beautiful curved buildings on each corner. In its day, the architecture of this street must have been stunning, but the complete lack of planning restrictions since has turned it into a grey mess compared to what it once was.

We were enjoying the views from our high vantage point when a group of young males join us at the top, they are fearless. Whilst we were carefully shuffling our way around the top of the minaret, never letting go of the railings, they are jumping from one side to the other, oblivious to the huge drop a mistimed landing could bring, that would be one fast route back down that spiral staircase! The size of the Mosque itself is appreciated even more from this vantage point, looking back down into the courtyard you can see how it is big enough to hold twenty-five thousand worshippers at any one time. Having looked across and down from all angles we make a steady journey back down, and are both relieved to get our feet planted back on terra firma. Time for one last wander around, a few more photographs, the handing over of the orange gown and its back to the car for the Red Fort via Chandni Chawk.

We may as well have walked; the journey was that short. Chaos is the first word that springs to mind when we remember Chandni Chawk, it is one of the oldest and busiest markets in Old Delhi and the streets just are not wide enough! Built just a few years after the Jama Masjid it was originally divided by canals and was known as Moonlight Square; it is hard to imagine these days of why it was given such a charming romantic name. Our five minutes here was more than enough to get a flavour (and smell) of this rat's nest of alleyways and lanes. It was no place to just stand, perpetual motion was going on all around us – we were in the way! You could have nightmares about getting yourself lost in the labyrinth of these narrow streets, you would not want to be delivering for Amazon and having to find your way around here...

The Red Fort is one of the places we just get to see rather than pay for entry. Our driver drops us off by the impressive Lahori Gate, right by the plaque celebrating India's independence. The guide gives us more dates and facts, the gate has this name as it was through here that the road led to Lahore, present day Pakistan. It was built, or at least commissioned by Shah Jahan as he moved his capital from Agra to Delhi, it was originally red and white and is still the centre piece of Independence Day celebrations on the fifteenth of August each year. Our visit is short and sweet, our photos are poor, the smog is worse than ever around here, and by now our eyes are beginning to feel sore.

With Old Delhi, or at least our itinerary for Old Delhi completed it is back to the car and on to New Delhi. The quantity of traffic had dissipated by now, but the journey is equally spell-binding. More goats, random dogs and open-backed trucks full of people and cargo that somehow defy gravity. Whoever is responsible for loading up some of these trucks and trailers must be the World Jenga Champion. Gradually the backdrop of the city changes, the roads become wider, tree lined and more cosmopolitan (well just a little).

India gate is our first stop, and like much of New Delhi it was designed by Edwin Lutyens and built in the 1920s. Although it is in the form of a gate it is best described as the Indian equivalent of our Cenotaph. It stands as a memorial to eighty-four thousand soldiers of the British Indian Army who lost their lives between 1914 and 1918 in the First World War - fighting anywhere from France to East Africa and across Asia. In looks it is very similar to, and is often compared in design to the Arc de Triomphe in Paris or the Gateway of India in Mumbai. The air seems cleaner here and some of the background noises of the constant car horns have disappeared, but that quiet is soon disturbed by a Kwality Walls Ice-cream tuk-tuk.

It is another short drive to Raj Ghat and the Gandhi memorial. Despite being right alongside a main road, this 'Garden of Peace' does provide a serene oasis in such a bustling city. It is a quite simple tribute to the father of India as we know him now. Sitting on a manicured lawn is a simple black marble plinth, square in shape and at the top end is a glass box containing an eternal flame lit within. While we are there some dignitaries are placing garlands of orange flowers on the stool at the foot of the stone. We are informed that this is the exact spot of where he was cremated, the day after his assassination.

Humayun's Tomb... We remember visiting here, but we could not remember a lot about the history, or even picture it at all. It was only when we looked at the photographs and DVD images that it came flooding back. It is a stunning shrine, with highly decorated ceilings, huge domes and magnificent carvings. Situated on the banks of a river it was the first garden tomb on the Indian sub-continent and was built upon the orders of a grieving partner with the instruction to create the finest mausoleum in the Mughal Empire - does that ring any bells yet? Ok, we are in Delhi on the banks of the Yamuna River, and this is considered the fore-runner to the Taj Mahal. Humayun's Tomb set a precedent for subsequent Mughal architecture which culminated in the Taj Mahal. Humayun was the second Mughal Emperor, so Shah Jahan's Great, Great Grandfather. Construction began in 1565 and took seven years to complete, and his grieving widow Empress Bega Begum footed the bill herself, a cool 1.5 million rupees! The design is inspired by Persian architecture but also incorporates several elements of Indian architecture.

With our heads spinning with all the information that we have tried to take in we do get a brief respite as we visit the heartland of Indias government. Our driver must drop us off and then move away, there is no parking allowed around these administrative buildings. Our guide walks us a short distance to where we can look through the gates and down a long path towards the Parliament building. It is a modern building and not especially Indian looking, more in common with European architecture than Asian. It was no surprise, in fact we guessed before the guide said, that it was another construction ordered by the British government, and once again Edwin Lutyens was behind it. The driveway down to the building has trees either side, uniformly spaced out, but what impressed us most was the topiary elephants at the end of the road nearest to us. Very impressive and undoubtedly a step up on a cockerel! The gates that we are peering through are also decorated with elephants on top of the pillars, adding an Indian flavour to what is a very British looking build. More information from the guide before he makes a quick phone call and summons our driver!

The final stop of the day takes us to Qutb Minar, home of the highest stone tower in the whole of India. It doesn't sound that exciting but as well as the tower there are plenty more remains to be seen in this park. The tower itself is carved and decorated at every point, so while with modern building techniques its size is not astounding the craftsmanship and the 'how did they do that?' factor is most definitely to be admired. Five storeys high and a mixture of both semi-circular curves and angles (flanged pilasters), twelve of each on the first four layers; Wikipedia says fluted and with 'superb stalactite bracketing under the balconies' - but that went a little over my head. The fifth storey is just circular these days but was originally part of the fourth storey - they were separated into two individual layers following a repair made necessary by a lightning strike in 1369.

The height of the Qutb Minar is a little over seventy-two metres, making it the tallest minaret in the world built of bricks. With a fourteen-metre base diameter that tapers to just under three metres at the very top it is only sixty-five centimetres out from being judged perfect by a laser light spirit level. That is some feat of engineering, especially when you take into consideration that it is eight hundred years old.

Whereas everything else of real age that we have seen today has been of Islamic design the Qutb Minar is considered as one of the earliest but also one of the best Hindu – Muslim fusions. Interestingly many of the mosques built in Delhi during this period had the minarets constructed by Hindu labourers and craftsmen, but all overseen by Muslim architects. Over the years it has been patched up, but much of the complex is just ruins. The 'Victory Tower' as it is also known remains as one of the most visited tourist spots in Delhi.

Our guide for the day had been superb, not only very knowledgeable in his facts and figures, but also charming throughout the day, pointing out the best places for photographs, telling us about his family and asking about ours. It was the bit we were dreading the 'tipping' moment. Perhaps it is us British, no one likes talking about tipping, how much is handed over is normally done discreetly and the actual amount never mentioned. The last thing we would ever want to do is leave him feeling insulted, or think that we had not thought he was very good, so we gave him a tip of ten pounds; from his reaction it is safe to say that was on the large side, between passing him the tip and getting back to the car we had been invited to his forthcoming wedding!

It is an early morning start for the four-hour plus journey to Agra, too early for a proper breakfast but we do get a pre-packed one from reception as we leave, a mix of fruits, bread and of course a hard-boiled egg. Breakfast in India without having an egg is unthinkable, even illegal...

Even though traffic is minimal at this time of the morning it seems a long while before we escape the confines, or at least the city sprawl of Delhi and its suburbs. Once it is in the rear mirror the roads are surprisingly good, dual carriageway for the most part and three lanes in some places. These faster roads are not without their hazards, cows are often asleep in the fast lane with their backs pressed tight up against the kerbside. There seems to be an unwritten rule where you are even allowed to drive on the wrong side of the road, if you keep flashing your lights; on two or three occasions there are tractors heading towards us on our side of the road. Dogs as hazards are suddenly the least of your problems, driving this route, especially in this type of light halfway between darkness and dawn must take every ounce of concentration. If we were not wide awake when we departed, we are now. The journey passes quickly, we felt far more comfortable once proper daylight arrived, and we even had time for a cup of tea at a plush service station on route.

With Agra in touching distance our first stop of the day is to visit Akbar's Tomb in Sikandra. It is another impressive building but not on the scale, or at least not of the size of Humayun's Tomb that we had visited yesterday. With no grieving widow to organise a more elaborate tribute, Akbar's resting place was built by his son Jahangir. Maybe it was a reluctance to spend his inheritance that held the grandeur back a little is our first thought, which is a shame as Akbar (the third Mughal Emperor), was known as Akbar the Great.

When I say things like 'not on the scale' or lacking the grandeur' that is not to say these aren't beautiful pieces of architecture, they undoubtedly are – if this had been the first Tomb that we had seen then our reaction would have been wow! For anyone who has ever done a safari it is like how excited you get when you see your first herd of zebras, four hours later you just drive past them with barely a second glance – stunning tombs and beautiful zebras, you do get blasé about them!

If the South Gateway through which we entered to visit Akbars tomb was simplistic, the ceilings on the insides were magnificent. The exterior is a construction of red sandstone with glossy white marble inlaid in geometric patterns, the white of the minarets shining brightly against the blue sky. The domed ceilings inside are beautifully inlaid with golds, russet hues and a mix of sky and dark blues, depicting grapes and leaves. In the grounds, best described as a symmetrical walled garden is the mausoleum itself. It is a five-tiered structure with each level going up getting smaller (think wedding cake); the central arch rises all the way up to the fourth floor as the centre piece, decorated with panels of marble and intricate carvings. Akbar's reign hugely influenced the course of Indian history, and during his reign the Mughal Empire tripled in size and wealth. He reformed and united the country by not only abolishing the sectarian tax on non-Muslims but also considering and appointing them to high level positions. It is safe to say that he was the first Mughal ruler to win the trust and loyalty of all the Indian people. The one blot on his copybook we will come to later, and maybe that explains why his son was a bit tight with his tomb, Akbar had wasted a lot of money...

The distance to Agra was now in single digits, so we were looking in all directions for that first glimpse of the Taj Mahal. If it was goats that were prevalent in Delhi, buffalo is the animal of choice here, farmer after farmer is marching his beasts down the roadside. What we could also see was that every other road side stall was selling motor cycle helmets, it seems impossible that they could all be making a living, how many crash hats does one person need? With no sign of the Taj Mahal our first impression of Agra is not a good one, traffic grinds to a halt as a mass brawl is going on in the road. Rocks are being thrown, and the locals are wielding sticks to hit each other with. Two or three tyres burning in the road and general mayhem all around us - our driver does well to navigate through a small gap and get beyond this neighbourly dispute. Welcome to Agra...

With our guide asking if we were hungry (it was by now a long time since breakfast), we get to experience some proper street food. Apart from breakfasts, all other meals on this trip are at our own expense, so rather than the two of us sit in some restaurant that the guide deemed suitable for tourists we convinced him that we would much prefer to eat from the food stalls lining the roads. With the Mughal influence on food around here, we tucked into shawarmas as well as samosas, treat the guide to his lunch and spent next to nothing. A far more enjoyable experience than being sat in a restaurant with more waiters than customers with our guide waiting outside, and us worrying about how much we should tip for the meal!

Fed and watered, Agra Fort is where we will spend the rest of the afternoon. Despite the local punch up that we witnessed earlier Agra is very tourist orientated. The sights and sound of flute playing snake charmers complete with the stereotypical wicker baskets greets us as we cross the road. In front of the fort there must be a dozen or more horse and carriages looking for business, tours of the city being offered by card waving drivers, luckily our guide is on hand and we get away without the hard sell. While the horse might be the animal of choice to transport sightseers around, it was the camel pulling huge trucks that was being used to shift goods from A to B. We had seen them on route between Delhi and Agra, but here we were in the heart of the city and they are being used everywhere.

It's that man Akbar who is behind Agra Fort, built between 1565 and 1573 and the size of fifty football pitches, or ninety-four acres in more technical terms. It is a majestic sandstone build, like a walled city - shaped like a crescent with its eastern wall flanked by the river Yamuna. It is our first visit inside an Indian 'castle,' and we are astonished by the sheer size of the place – not just its footprint but more the width and height of the gateways and arches within. Our guide gives us a simple explanation, and we immediately feel a little dumb for not having realised why... In the United Kingdom, (and right across Europe), soldiers would ride to fight to battle on horseback – and that governs how high arches etc need to be. In this part of the world, whilst they did use horses why stop there? Elephants were far more resilient, readily available and could quite literally be used to crush the enemy – especially if they only had mere horses.

There were originally four entrances that allowed access, two of which have since been walled up, and only one is open to the public these days – the Lahore gate. Disappointingly, what is considered the finest gate is out of bounds to visitors; the Delhi gate was the Kings formal gate, highly decorated in white marble and with a wooden drawbridge over the moat that was guarded by two life-sized stone elephants, complete with their riders. We would have loved to seen those huge statues but unfortunately due to that part of the fort still being used by the Indian military it is completely out of reach to tourists, which seems a real shame.

Once we are inside our guide gives us more information about elephant proofing the fort from attack. When we had passed through the entrance gateway, we never really noticed the fact that there was almost immediately a ninety-degree corner, and a towering wooden gate, we were gazing up at the high walls and appreciating the shade from the sun that they gave. The design is like this for two main reasons; firstly, elephants have a large turning circle and secondly, they need a good run up to build up speed. So, this is a perfect defence mechanism - enemy forces are slowed right down by the right-angled bends, and then even once they are through that, the huge wooden gate is right upon them before the elephant can get enough pace up to use its weight to bulldoze its way through.

Whilst from the outside Agra Fort is an imposing stone structure once you get inside you cannot help but be impressed with the beauty of the buildings contained within. By now we have navigated our way through the dog-leg bends and the whole place opens out into a huge courtyard. The first thing that captures your eye as you enter is Jehangir Mahal, a palace said to have been built by Akbar solely for the women to bathe in. Simple but elegant, it is home to a large stone bowl upon which are carved Persian verses and allegedly this used to be filled with a constant supply of rose water. Opposite to here lies the palace built for Jodha Bai, said to be Akbar's favourite queen.

At one time there used to be around five hundred buildings in this walled city, but today less than thirty survive. Shah Jahan destroyed many within the first hundred years of the fort as he made room for his white marble palaces. One of Shah Jahan's early palaces remains, modestly naming after himself - Shahjahani Mahal. It has a big hall, with side rooms and an octagonal tower facing towards the river. Against the red sandstones of the fort this palace is hugely different, glimmering white plaster but colourfully painted with floral designs. Most of the others were destroyed by the British troops of East India Company between 1803 and 1862, simply wiping out much of the finest Mughal architecture ever known just to make more room for their soldiers to train on the newly created parade ground...

Looking through the photo albums, the part of the fort that we both instantly recalled was the summer palace, another addition to the fort made by Shah Jahan. To give the palace its correct title (which we would not have remembered) is the Sheesh Mahal, which translates to the 'Palace of Mirrors.' The walls of this palace are incredibly thick, helping to keep it cool in even the highest of temperatures – but it is the mosaics made of high-quality mirrors adorning both its walls and ceilings that make this an unforgettable sight. Thousands of individual pieces of glass and mirror were brought from Haleb, (now known as Aleppo), in Syria. These were then painstakingly attached individually creating the magical effect and patterns that survive to this day. There is little wonder that this single palace took nine years (1631 – 1640) to build, the whole fort only took eight! In its day, this room of glass and mirrors would have been illuminated, giving a sparkling effect to the entire palace, not a bad place for the emperor to have a bath!

Finally... we get our first glimpse of the Taj Mahal! What these days is a stunning palace made from white marble was originally built of red stone by Akbar who used it to watch the sunrise every day. It is situated overlooking the riverside, facing towards the East. The original sandstone building was replaced by the current structure favoured by Shah Jahan around 1632-1640. It is a large complex with lots of rooms and little alcoves, deep niches on the walls of the bigger hall break up the monotony of the length. The centre pillars, brackets and lintels bear exquisite designs and carvings and it is recognised as one of the most magnificent buildings of Shah Jahan. With a majestic view looking across the river of the Taj Mahal it is quite ironic that Shah Jahan spent the last eight years of his life imprisoned in this complex, (1658-1666). Upon his death his body was taken by boat to the Taj Mahal and he was reunited with his favourite wife, Mumtaz Mahal.

After leaving the Agra Fort our guide had the driver take us on a short drive running the entire length of the fort wall, just to get some idea of the scale. We then turned off and went down to the river Yamuna where we pulled over and took a few photographs, navigating the rubbish and stench from the polluted river to capture a few images at dusk of this world-famous monument to love...

The big day had arrived, this morning we would visit the Taj Mahal, the centre piece, or main selling point, of the Golden Triangle. Yesterday afternoon we had seen it in the distance from Agra Fort but today we would be exploring it properly. The usual early start, and the usual fog, the now familiar routine of meeting the driver in reception before the short drive to the Taj itself. I am not sure exactly what we were expecting but we were taken by surprise by the number of people about at this time of the morning, both visitors and street vendors. Already the queues were on the long side. We were entertained by the monkeys running along the perimeter walls while we kept gently shuffling along as the queue was moving. Before going in we had to split up to pass through the security scanners, just like at airports here, males to one side, females the other.

Having got in there was still no sign of the Taj Mahal, instead more gardens before you eventually come to the gateway from where you catch your first sight. We could see the domes, but unfortunately the fog was still lingering about, hopefully as the morning passes the sun would disperse that? Our guide moves us on through the gate and takes us to a quieter area before telling us all about it, and then we are left to our own devices to go and explore it for ourselves.

A brief history (and appreciate that many of you may already know) ... Taj Mahal translates as 'Crown of the Palace' and is of Indo-Islamic design. It was commissioned in 1632 by Shah Jahan to house the tomb of his favourite wife, Mumtaz Mahal who had died in labour giving birth to their fourteenth child the previous year. Located on the southern bank of the river Yamuna in Agra it is constructed from white marble and built upon a square plinth, symmetry being at the heart of the design. The four minarets on each corner of the base are slightly angled so that in the event of an earthquake they would fall away from the domed roof. The tomb itself is recognised as being the best-preserved example of Mughal architecture and it is also one of the most recognisable buildings in the world. The mausoleum is 'just' the centre piece of the complex that also contains a Mosque and a guesthouse and is surrounded on three sides by a sandstone wall, the river itself providing the fourth boundary. Outside of these walls are further mausoleums to Shah Jahan's other wives, the ones who were just ok....

The cost did not come cheap, from being commissioned in 1632, the mausoleum itself, (what we recognise as the Taj Mahal), was completed in 1643. Work on the gardens and the rest of the complex went on for a further ten years. The total bill was around thirty-two million rupees, in modern day terms that is estimated at around one billion US dollars. One of the myths about the place is that the architects and craftsmen were deliberately blinded, (or even murdered), following its completion on the orders of Shah Jahan. The story goes that he wanted to make sure that they could play no part in the creation of another building that would ever match the beauty of the Taj; no concrete evidence has ever been found to support this claim.

The fog had turned more to a hazy mist and was gradually clearing as we wandered up the tree lined paths towards the Taj Mahal, its dome mirrored in the reflecting pool halfway along. It is from this point we got our best photograph which was hung up in our hallway for years; the Taj Mahal itself was less of the attraction but more being used as the backdrop, the reflections of dozens of Indian ladies in their finest brightly coloured clothes reflecting beautifully in the water were the stars of the show.

Upon reaching the square base of the building you must put on overshoes to protect the floors from damage before proceeding any further. So, with our footwear shrouded in a bright orange overshoe we head up the steps to get closer and really appreciate the work and detail of this famous building. The decorative painted elements are a mix of scriptures - passages from the Qur'an, and depictions of flowers and vines. Carvings add texture to the smooth curved arches and insets. The minarets and dome are just a simple brickwork design which contrasts perfectly with the elegantly decorated panels, and the latticework featuring Islamic symbols provides a mix of light and shadows to the interior of the structure. On each corner of the edifice are small chattris, (little kiosks), with domed roofs that keeps the uniformity of the whole design. Perched on top of the main thirty-five metre dome is a gold-coloured finial topped by a moon, a standard Islamic motif. We venture inside where the inlay work continues, octagonal in shape and with a false ceiling it is a place of calm. The four upper arches form balconies, and each of the exterior windows have an intricate screen cut from marble. Every surface is decorated or inlaid with semi-precious stones forming twining vines, fruits and flowers. With such attention to detail and precision you can see why it took twenty thousand skilled craftsmen ten years to create this masterpiece.

What is left of the mist refuses to give into the sun, so although it has lifted a fair bit since we arrived there is no sign of a blue sky, so disappointingly we have not seen the Taj Mahal at its finest. They say the dome reflects different colours throughout the day, but despite being there from opening time we have not been fortunate enough to witness that, but we have still enjoyed our visit. With a final look over our shoulders we take a final glance before heading back to the car, Jaipur is our next destination, the best part of five hours away. On route we will visit what was Akbar the Greats new capital city, or at least until its abandonment a few years later...

Fatehpur Sikri was somewhere that we had never heard of, but it turned out to be one of our favourite parts of the whole tour. Situated between Agra and Jaipur it is the city that never was. They built a stunning array of buildings but then soon discovered that they had no natural water supply, so it was swiftly abandoned. It was a strange eerie experience; you could see the grandeur of the place but the reality was that more tourists have walked around these buildings than anyone else, it was never used as it was intended. There were plenty of shady areas and the steps seemed to be covered by a combination of sleeping dogs and climbing goats. In the distance there was a tower where his favourite elephant had been buried, now digging that hole would have been no easy feat!

A city existed here long before Akbar appointed it as his capital, in fact Humayun had already done much to redesign Fatehpur Sikri's layout. The main attraction of here was the opportunity to get away from the noise and chaos of Agra yet still have the benefits of its proximity. It was well linked both by boat and land. It was founded as the capital of the Mughal empire by Akbar in 1571 and served this role for just fourteen years, more in name only, before being completely abandoned in 1610. The exact reason for its failure is usually put down do a failure to secure a water supply, but the alternative theory is that Akbar developed and extended it on a whim, wanting to build his own city rather than continuing his rule from Agra.

Fatehpur Sikri nestles upon a rocky ridge, bordered by a near four-mile wall on three sides with the fourth naturally created by a lake. The city is perched on this forty-metre-high ridge, and falls into the shape of a rhombus. The general layout of the remaining structures leads urban archaeologists to conclude that Fatehpur Sikri was built primarily to afford leisure and luxury to its famous residents, a rich man's playground. Like Agra it was built from red sandstone, while the architecture reflects both Hindu and Muslim design of the time. Amongst all the red stone is just one exception, the tomb of Salim Chishti; he was the saint who predicted the birth of Akbar's son. This mausoleum was constructed by Akbar as a thank you; built upon a platform the entrance is reached by a handful of steps and made from white marble. The walls are not solid but more a fine mesh, allowing the light to permeate inside. The tomb is in the centre of the main hall, which has a single semi-circular dome. Unusually, or at least it is the first time that we have seen, it is adorned with mosaics of black and yellow marble, arranged in geometric patterns. A wooden canopy with a gold roof is the centre piece and locals walk around, touching the green cloth and leaving garlands.

Everything else in the whole complex is sandstone red, there are ornate finishes to the eaves and carvings on pillars, but not another colour in sight apart from a tiny glimpse of white on domed roofs, pigeon deposits? Even the huge pond in the centre has sandstone bridges running across it, this place is very different to anywhere else we have seen on this tour. The gate we entered through is the most embellished feature of the whole place, grand arches and then multiple domes running along the top. The Panch Mahal, or five-level palace, is very understated – an open series of pillars forming a square on each of the levels, each layer going up smaller in size like a Lego pyramid. Everything looks incredibly open plan, but our guide informs us that in its day the 'glamour' would have come from the decoration of the interiors, the massive halls being partitioned with ornate screens.

Now, obviously I have not just remembered all these facts, I have been reading the guides and doing some further research to paint the story behind these places, (rather than just a token list of all the places we visited). By doing all this digging around I have stumbled across my first disappointment, the tower that our guide pointed out as the burial site of Akbar's favourite elephant... that may well be nonsense. Experts suggest that it may just have been a starting point for subsequent mile posts, how boring is that?

Our hotel in Jaipur was stunning. We stayed at the Umaid Bhawan, they brand it as a Heritage hotel, and it was truly amazing, the doors were simply works of art and would not have been out of place if they had been in the City Palace that we would visit tomorrow. Every corridor and stairway had you spellbound, beautiful antique furnishings, artwork adorning the walls, and finally we reach our door and turn the key... our room did not disappoint! The biggest double bed that we have ever slept in, but all around the outside of this huge room was a raised floor covered with cushions and drapes, there would have been enough room for me to have a whole harem in this place. At the foot of the bed was the lounge area, a lovely dark wooden sofa with a pair of chairs, only the modern flatscreen TV ruined the style of the décor. The bathroom was equally as opulent, a massive bath that you could almost swim in and the sink and mirrors so ornate. It is safe to say that the bathroom alone was bigger than most of the rooms that we have stayed in. With us having arrived late afternoon / early evening we even have time to make use of the swimming pool. The courtyard that surrounds it is in keeping with the rest of the property; paintings of Maharajas from the past on pale blue turreted walls give a nod to the part of the country that you are in. To this day we have never spent time in a better hotel, some may have been more luxurious, full of all mod cons - here just felt so special.

First stop of the day for us was the Amber Fort, about seven miles out of Jaipur, in a small town called Amer from where it takes its name. Amer, that is not a typing error, it is just that us tourists all know it as the Amber Fort (or even Amber Palace), perhaps because of the similarity of the colour in certain light, or even a play on the name? The red sandstone of Delhi and Agra have been replaced with pale yellow and pink sandstone, a little lighter on the colour chart. The Mughal Emperors have also gone, this is the land of the Rajput Maharajas. We thought Agra Fort was huge, but this is on another level, the ramparts of the fort are towering high above Lake Maota, dwarfing it to the size of a pond in comparison. Walls attached to the fort disappear over hills into the distance, the boundaries of this place are further than the eye can see. Even before we have got out of the car we are in awe of this place, what a building!

The itinerary for us includes the elephant ride up to the fort walls, this is not something that we would do these days, being more aware of how elephants are abused in their 'training' regime. Indeed, our experience on the day itself was not pleasant at all, and left us with one horrible memory from what is otherwise a beautiful place. After about an hour's wait in the heat it was our turn to 'board' an elephant for the ride up to the fort itself. Dozens of elephants are making endless circular trips up and down these cobbled paths, and they are prone to overtake each other. Factor in an elephant making its way back down and there is no room for three abreast - it was at this point when our mahout cracked the elephant over the head with a metal bar to bring it in check. I guess the ride from start to end is about fifteen minutes in all, it was not particularly comfortable for us, we had quickly discovered that elephants have a continuous rolling motion, you are constantly having to brace yourself. Compared to our relative discomfort though, the elephant had taken one hell of a crack to its head.

Our guide met us at the top and proceeded to tell us all about the place, of how self-sufficient it was in its day and its multiple innovative features. The town of Amer and the Amber Fort were built by Raja Man Singh in 1592 but further progressed under Sawai Jai Singh. Located high on a hill the fort overlooks Maota Lake, which provides its main source of water. The lake has an island in the centre, where fruit and vegetables would have been grown, irrigated by using the water from the lake to provide food for the residents. The lake had one other important use, helping to create a more pleasant climate within the fort itself by providing the source for water features and cascades. Having cold water running between the rooms and courtyards meant the hot winds would feel just that little cooler.

The courtyard that we have been delivered to is huge, I guess it is back to the horse versus elephant scale scenario again, this makes even the biggest castles that we have visited back home look like a folly! At any one point there are perhaps twenty or so elephants wandering around, setting down tourists before heading back down the cobbled walkways to pick up their next load. It is a spectacular sight, all the elephants are decked in bright colours; covered by a red throw with a thick blue band around the outside, trimmed with a thin beading of gold between the two colours, they do look amazing. The 'customers' are perched in a box shaped structure, all looking as awkward as we felt, riding the constant tilting and rolling of these huge beasts. The mahouts sitting on the neck of the elephant look surprisingly comfortable, perhaps that is a more stable position?

With the size of this place, you could easily spend the entire day here, so with a packed schedule our guide whisks us off for what we suspect is an edited highlights tour; reassuringly though, in research for writing this book we have visited all the places of importance. In this first courtyard is one of the most decorated buildings we have ever seen (it feels like we have been saying that every day!), the Ganesh Pol entrance. It takes its name from the Hindu god Lord Ganesh, who legend has it removes all obstacles in life, this is the entrance into the private palaces of the Maharajas. It is a three-level structure with many frescoes, and above this gate is the Suhag Mandir where ladies of the royal family used to watch functions held in the courtyard through the latticed marble windows. It is hard to describe the beauty of this building, absolute symmetry on a creamy yellow stoned building, decorated in reds, jade, black and russets. There is not a panel that has been neglected, the archways and ceilings are especially ornate, triangular patterns and silver stars providing a feast for the eyes.

We walk by the Sila Devi temple and admire its double door covered in silver with a raised relief. Inside here are two lions made of silver, but more impressive, but less shiny is the carving of Lord Ganesha, which is made from a single piece of coral. This is also where animal sacrifice during important festivals would take place, usually a buffalo but also goats, all in the presence of the royal family. These days though, animal sacrifice has been replaced with offerings made to the goddess being of the vegetarian type, no more buffalo, a butternut squash...?

Up the steps to the second courtyard, but not much to see here, an audience hall on a raised platform, nice columns but not much more to say. More steps and we reach the third - the private quarters of the Maharaja, via the servant's route! The courtyard here has just two buildings, built opposite each other but separated by a garden laid out in the fashion of the Mughal Gardens. A star shaped pool in the centre and with octagonal beds separated by water channels is my best attempt at describing it. The first of the two is the Jai Mandir, or the Sheesh Mahal (Mirror Palace) – the second of those we have come across in three days! This one is even more impressive though, exquisitely embellished glass inlaid panels and ceilings as before but the coloured foils add that little extra. There is no wonder it is looking so pristine, spoiler alert – it is virtually brand new. If that took the gloss off what we had just seen, the vista of the lake and island gardens below quickly make you forget, the view from up here is stunning. The second building is the Sukh Mahal, the erotically named Hall of Pleasure. Far more discreet, entry is through a sandalwood door and the walls are decorated with simple marble inlay. The main interest in here is more the piped water supply flowing through an open channel keeping the hall cool, like an early day air-conditioning system.

Continuing our upward momentum, we reach the fourth, and final, courtyard. This fourth courtyard is where the women of the Royal family live... and that includes the king's concubines or mistresses in modern day language. The living quarters here was designed to give the king a full choice of his lovers, but without alerting any of the other occupants to which lady he was visiting; all the rooms opened from a single common corridor – makes it sound like a seventeenth century Travelodge. The oldest part of the palace fort, to the south of this courtyard is the Palace of Man Singh I, this took twenty-five years to build and was completed in 1599. In the central courtyard of the palace is a pavilion; used as the meeting venue by the maharanis (the queens of the royal family). Access from this palace leads to nearby Jaigarh Fort (not one we get to visit), but also to the nearby town of Amer. A series of underground tunnels had been built to provide an escape route, so if ever the fort was under threat safe passage and a quick getaway was to hand.

With that our tour of here was complete, it was time to navigate the stairs and passages all the way back down to the bottom. As if to emphasise the sheer scale of this fort we pass by the biggest curry pots that we have ever seen; both of us could have bathed in it at once. Even more bizarre was the fact that it had a handle on either side, just like a standard Balti dish – good luck to whoever was trying to lift that! You would need a naan bread the size of a mattress to mop that one out...

Next item on our itinerary takes us on the short journey back to Jaipur - the City Palace is our next stop. Before we reach the city confines, we stop on route to view the Water Palace, or the Jal Mahal to give it its proper title. Set in the Man Sager Lake only the top floor is visible, the other four floors are submerged under the water, and despite a lot of time and money being spent on restoration access to your average tourist looks as far away as ever. Zooming in with your camera is as close a view as you can get.

Returning to Jaipur through one of its three city gates and we can instantly appreciate why it goes by the name of the pink city. It is built from the usual red sandstone but ever since 1876 it has always been painted a terracotta-pink colour. Queen Victoria's son, Albert, the Prince of Wales (who went on to became King Edward VII, and Emperor of India) visited that year, and with pink being the colour of hospitality at the time, the whole city was painted that shade for his welcome. It was Prince Albert who was said to have described Jaipur as the 'pink city,' coining the name that Jaipur is still known by today.

To our left is the Hawa Mahal, the Palace of the Winds – five stories high and too big to get in shot without cables ruining the picture! It is the most iconic building in Jaipur, certainly one that we could put a name to without the help of our guide. This pink gem is a five-story structure that thins out to the width of a single room by the time you are on the third floor - the first and second floors have patios in front of them. Seen from the street it is like a honeycomb with bay windows alternating between small and large. Each 'window,' there is no glass, has carved sandstone grills, finials and domes, providing a very distinctive look. From the front façade there are 953 niches, each with intricately carved openings. Its design is said to be a fusion of Hindu Rajput architecture with Islamic Mughal; so, as well as enjoying marriages between these two great powers they also pooled ideas when creating buildings. The cooling effect in the chambers, provided by the breeze passing through the small windows provided the perfect place to allow royal ladies to observe everyday life and festivals in the street below without being seen. Many people see the Hawa Mahal from the street view and think it is the front of the palace, but it is actually the back.

The streets are chaotic here, looking back at a couple of minutes of our video footage and there are carts being pulled by oxen, horses and small tractors. Monkeys climb across the city gates and cows are eating from the piles of swept up rubbish. Just for good measure there are a few chickens wandering around and a pair of brightly dressed snake charmers, Jaipur is the first Indian city that we have really enjoyed wandering around. Rather than tight little alleys the roads are wide, and for the first time on this tour the sky is blue, the relaxed atmosphere of here is something that we never found in either Delhi or Agra.

The City Palace was established at the same time as the city of Jaipur in 1727. To this day Jaipur is the capital of the state of Rajasthan, and up until 1949 the City Palace was the ceremonial and administrative seat of the Maharaja. It continues to be the home of the Jaipur royal family, so access to the palace is limited. After our mornings exertions there is still plenty for us to view and more dates, names and maharajas than we can ever remember! There are three gates to the complex, one strictly for special visitors, not the likes of us

– but from a distance we can get a good look at it. The gates that the public use is not too shabby either; arches, gates and doors are never likely to be built like this again, the craftwork and beauty of the intricate details put into these would never happen these days. Once inside the courtyard our guide has us lined up for a photograph alongside the palace guards, they all look magnificent in their white tunics with gold buttons, the uniform topped off with red turbans and of course they are all sporting the obligatory moustache. Amazingly they do not even ask for a tip!

It is the doorways that we are drawn too, some are towering way above us with white marble carvings or lattice work, others are painted depicting peacocks with their tail feathers fanned out. Our guide explains how this represent the four seasons and Hindu gods, it is the Peacock gate we are looking at, representing autumn and Lord Vishnu. As we wander around, we come to the Lotus Gate (a continual flower and petal pattern) for summer and Lord Shiva; a very green gate, depicting spring and dedicated to Lord Ganesha, and finally the Rose Gate (more flowers) for the winter season and dedicated to Goddess Devi. We feel that the guide is on a mission and we are swiftly moved on inside to the museum. A silver urn, one of a pair, and as tall as us is on display - at over five foot in height it is in the book of Guinness World Record as the world's largest sterling silver vessel. Made from fourteen thousand melted silver coins, these were specially commissioned by Maharaja Sawai Madho Singh II to carry the water of the Ganges to drink on his trip to England in 1902. Now I am not certain of the state of the Ganges way back then, but I certainly would not fancy drinking from it these days …

One of the oldest buildings in the complex is the Chandra Mahal. Spread over seven floors, a number considered auspicious by Rajput rulers, it has two notable features... the first two floors consist of the Sukh Niwas, the House of pleasure - that is the second one of those we have seen, make of that what you will? There is a second stunning (different?) room that jumps out at you - called Chhavi Niwas with its blue and white decorations. The blue is a dark blue, so very bold compared to a lot of the more subtle pastel shades that we have seen in the last few days. It is like Laurence Llewelyn-Bowen has been given a room to have a crack at, completely out of character with the rest of the building. The roof has the royal standard of Jaipur hoisted at all times, and when the Maharaja is in residence there is also a quarter flag (the same design, but a quarter of the size).

With so much information our minds are at bursting point, but there is still no sign of our guide easing up. Next stop is just around the corner, and to be fair we had about had enough! Jantar Mantar, (as well as rhyming), is a collection of huge stone built astronomical instruments. Created in the early eighteenth century by Maharaja Jai Singh II, the primary purpose of the observatory was to compile astronomical tables and to predict the times and movements of the sun, moon and planets. Not content with having one observatory he went on to create another four - New Delhi, Ujjain, Mathura and Varanasi.

Rajah Jai Singh II had a keen interest in mathematics, architecture and astronomy and with these massive instruments that he had ordered to be built a skilled observer could tell the time to an accuracy of about two seconds using the declination of the Sun and the other heavenly bodies. It is still (and likely to remain) the world's largest stone sundial, known as the Vrihat Samrat Yantra. Meaning 'supreme instrument' it consists of a gigantic triangular gnomon (the part that casts the shadow), a hypotenuse parallel to the Earth's axis and a quadrant of a circle, parallel to the plane of the equator. This was just one of the instruments, but the only one we could instantly relate to. By now our brains were frazzled, we didn't appreciate this part of the tour as much as we should. I imagine if we had started the tour here, fresh and recharged then we would have been more receptive to what each part was for, but unfortunately, we were tired and ready for a break. Our itinerary even extended into the evening today, although we were promised the next part would be a lot lighter, even fun filled...

Chokhi Dhani Village, the perfect antidote to what had been a weary day. Cerebrally we were drained, so a trip to a mock Rajasthani village for food and traditional entertainment should be a welcome light-hearted part of the trip. The sounds from the drums could be heard even before we entered, a noisy evening was awaiting us. It turns out to be a great night, mainly local families (or at least domestic tourists), and a smattering of white faces as we wander around, the most taxing part of the evening was sitting cross-legged for us! Food was served, it is cushions on the floor and a table one foot off the ground which is soon overflowing with plates and bowls that is an absolute feast. A great experience but we are nothing like as nimble as our fellow diners, it does take some getting back up, especially with a full stomach.

The village has a handful of shops that we wander around, it is an opportunity to see what colour turban suits me best! Despites the sales lady best efforts I leave empty-handed, Alison cannot be convinced either that the local outfits would be suitable for back home. Outside the entertainment is in full swing, traditional dancing on one stage but we are more fascinated by the sword swallowing act – not content with having one down his throat, he then proceeds to balance the sword stand on his chin. I think the constant drumming would have put me off. Young children are being whisked around the site in the back of a cart pulled by a huge white ox or having their photographs taken next to models of villagers with upturned moustaches. For some mad reason I end up having a massage. What starts off with a head massage turns to a monkey scrub and vigorous ear pulling before he finally moves down to my shoulders. With the head part finished for the second time this evening I find myself modelling a turban as my masseuse works on my shoulders - he does not hold back as his burly hands squeeze and pummel them before pulling both arms right behind my back, and using his elbow gets right between the shoulder blades. I am not sure at what point massage becomes an assault; it must have been close – but I must say I did feel invigorated by it!

With our evening over we are returned to our hotel, and it is time for a beer! The bottles of Kingfisher here are nothing like as cheap as in Goa, but still a bargain compared to a beer back home. Tonight, we are unwinding – our tour of the Golden Triangle is complete, and we have loved every minute of it. All that is left is to navigate that one final journey, a six-hour drive back to Delhi and our onward flight to Goa.

It is on the final drive of our journey that we have our funniest moment. It is a long drive from Jaipur back to Delhi and after a couple of hours or so our driver pulls into a service station, well I use that term loosely. It is nothing like the one that we visited on route between Delhi and Agra, that had table service, and the prices on your menu differed depending on if you were local or a tourist... This 'service station' was more a handful of tables and mismatched chairs outside a small roadside building. The cups of tea were excellent, milky and sweet, served in random chipped mugs, but that is not a problem to us at all. The comedy began when our driver pointed to the toilets, it had been two hours on the road already, so whilst not bursting it is a good time to go as we've still a long time to go before we reach the airport.

The toilets looked more like a cow shed, it was built from a combination of brickwork and corrugated steel, but it is what it is. Alison went first, disappeared around the other side before reappearing within twenty seconds, she obviously was not that desperate to go! Without doubt us men get it easier on the toilet front, most of the time it is just stand up and aim, so I was not deterred. In fact, as I walked between the wall and the corrugated sheet, I was pleasantly surprised, there was a proper urinal hanging on the wall! It was a little wet around the ground underneath so I stood a little further back than was normal, trusting my aim. Within a second or two of me relieving myself urine started splattering against the floor – suddenly standing well back was an incredibly wise decision, otherwise I would just have soaked my own feet with pee! There may well have been a urinal attached to the wall, and with that few seconds of delay before my pee hit the floor, I suspect there might also have even been a U bend... but that was where the plumbing had finished. I walked back to Alison chuckling to myself; celebrating having kept my feet dry...

Safely delivered to the airport and it is time to tip the driver, he was the guy who has been our constant companion throughout the five days. Whilst he might only speak very limited English, and obviously is not as educated as the guides, it is his hands who our lives have been in for hundreds of miles. How do you balance up the worth of passing on knowledge and information against the concentration and skill of navigating roads shared with plenty of crazy drivers and sleeping, mooing hazards? I know for certain that I would not want to drive on these roads and have such responsibility. It is safe to say that he was happy with what we gave him, and even if he were about to enter matrimonial bliss, he would not have spoken enough English to give us our second wedding invite of the trip...

Having survived hundreds of miles covering the Golden Triangle it is back in Goa where we experience our most hair-raising journey yet. It had always been the tour operators' bus for us upon our arrival at Dabolim airport, this time we need to arrange our own onward transport, so book a taxi from the set price kiosk at the airport. With a cab paid for we are given a slip of paper and told where to go, a driver will collect us in a few minutes. Talk about hanging on for dear life, we were both gripping the seat so tight that our knuckles were white, using just our hands alone that still was not enough - our legs were pushed hard into the floor to help brace us in an upright position. This guy was in a hurry, no doubt the sooner he could drop us off then he could get back and pick up another fare. Thankfully, we arrived back in one piece, and no we did not give him a tip.

Checking back in at the Senhor Angelo and we have been given a different room, we were not expecting to have moved but this one has a balcony overlooking the pool so we see it as quite an upgrade. Having got ourselves showered and smartened up we see the usual crowd are already by the pool bar; time to catch up with what everyone else has been up to and share our experiences from the last few days before we all head off in our separate ways for food. After eating we spend an hour (or two) in Madhu's before heading back towards the Senhor Angelo, it has been a long day and had been an early start so we are planning an early night... Those plans are thrown out of the window when we are walking back home past the Cricketers and see the rest of the pool bar crowd, the additional company along with a second wind means that we have a later than intended night, and even see us enjoying an evening where karaoke is involved – something that we always avoid (no we didn't / cannot sing). There is something about our first night back in resort, we always seem to end up hammered! A combination of tiredness and excitement, the smooth taste of Old Monk and Honey Bee, definitely.

A couple of other evenings we also headed down to the beach, the first time was just for a drink, but on the second occasion we had the suckling pig that we had ordered the night before at the Rovers Return, and what a spread that was! The pig was presented with its head on a platter, the banquet continued with mash and roast potatoes, cauliflower cheese, cabbage, gravy and apple sauce. The pork was cooked to perfection by Joseph (the shack owner), and the crackling was just sublime. It is amazing the quality of food that can be served up with what we would consider limited resources. I am led to believe that Joseph rears the pigs himself, so they are in his sole care from birth all the way through to the eating. The only downside of eating or drinking on the beach at night is that we were not overly keen on the walk back along the beach in darkness.

Another first on this trip was our discovery of the guy selling samosas, fried chillies etc by the Red Lion pub; that soon became part of the routine on the way back from a day at the beach. We got to know the time he arrived and fired up, so we made sure our departure from the beach was set to coincide with his fat hitting the correct temperature. Fresh samosas and a beer or two were just the job before we finished our walk back to the hotel. The young lad, Frankie, who worked at the Red Lion was more than happy for you to eat food at their tables, I guess the longer he could keep you in there drinking, the happier his boss was, and the more tips he would receive.

Alternating days on the beach, (always at the Rovers Return shack), with days around the pool worked perfectly for us. It was without doubt one of our most memorable holidays, we had ticked off something that we had always wanted to do, and with it being so full on it left us so tired and in need of rest that we thoroughly enjoyed the beach and pool, doing nothing other than relax – something that we often struggle with. Our evenings had also settled into a regular pattern, on our first visit we had been looking to do a pub crawl and have a drink in a few different places – this year our evening entertainment was a plastic chair and wooden table at Madhu's, the perfect place to watch the cows and traffic pass by late into the night. This was a Goan holiday template that worked for us and one that we would use time and again.

December 2011 - Goa and Hampi

For our third visit it was our third different hotel. We had booked through Thomas Cook this time, the Monarch flight from a year earlier was still too fresh in our memories for us to consider booking through Jewel in the Crown again. It is such a shame as we had loved our stay at the Senhor Angelo. I cannot remember what our hotel options were this time, but we chose the Mira Hotel knowing exactly where it was, an ideal location, just a short distance from our favourite restaurants, bars and within close proximity to the beach. For anyone not familiar with it, or maybe it's even changed its name over the last few years, it is close to the roundabout at the town end of the Beach Road, the one by Redondo's. Disappointingly the Thai restaurant that used to be attached to the Mira had gone, albeit not too far away.

Our daughter Lauren had been booked to come with us on this holiday, so because of that we had no internal flights booked on this occasion. When we had returned home the previous year with fake Radley handbags, glittering souvenirs etc, Lauren had decided that Goa was for her after all, so having turned down the opportunity on the last couple of occasions she was as keen as anything... Hampi would provide us with three days away from Goa – still leaving us plenty of days left for pool and beach time, keep her happy! When the time came for paying off the balance, she had had second thoughts; I don't like curry, I get heat rash, I will be bored at night... They were all true, so while we were out of pocket with losing the deposit for her booking it would be recouped over the time we were away.

This was the closest to Christmas that we had ever visited, in fact we returned home on Christmas Eve. Reception had the tree and decorations up, even the portrait of the lady who we think was the original owner of the hotel, displayed in pride of place at reception was decked out with tinsel. Our arrival in the dead of the night meant that the travel rep had to wake up the night security guy who was fast asleep on the floor behind the counter - the pair of 'guard' dogs were equally as alert, stretched out on the cool tiled floor. The room we had been given at the Mira was right at the front of the building, facing the road. Getting to sleep at night would be fine, the local spirits would see to that, but the noise in the morning started so early! There were a few mornings where we would be sat on the balcony; heads a little fuzzy still, but enjoying watching the world, and some huge rats, go by.

The hotel dog quota was high; as well as the reception pair there was another couple round by the pool and dining area. Breakfast was served down the side of the building, well within earshot of the neighbouring property where someone noisily cleared their throat of phlegm without fail every morning. We do not even remember eggs being an option here, (but with the phlegm issue that might have been a good thing), it was just toast and tea or coffee. There was a nice compact pool area, but unfortunately not much of it was in the sun. What we had noticed though, another block of rooms around the back of the hotel, overlooking the pool – that was to come in handy next year!

One of the first things we did was get our Hampi excursion booked through Valerie Travels, from memory that excursion is only available on two days a week, or at least it is by train. So, with that sorted it was down to the beach. Looking through the photographs it is the busiest we have ever seen the sand and sea. At the bottom of the Calangute steps and to the right it was heaving with people, the fumes from jet skis hanging in the air. In front of us were domestic tourists paddling in the sea, the guy's just in their underwear and the ladies still wearing everything, sarongs floating on the incoming waves!

We are all for the quieter life, so take a left turn and head towards our old haunt of the Rovers Return. As soon as you get a hundred metres away from the steps the crowds begin to thin out, the air is more pleasant and in no time, you reach the fishing boats that are rolled up the beach each day using logs to drag them away from the tide changes. The boats are bright red, with their name, Jolly Boys written in white, they must only have just got back in as the fishermen are still emptying their catch - they make for a great photo opportunity. We watch for a short while before heading just that little further on, eager for our first beer of the day. The yellow signage and sunbeds of the Rovers is soon within sight, so with a cold Kingfisher each and a sunbed for the afternoon, we pass our time by just watching the entertainment. Today's highlight was when a family of three set up their own 'trapeze' wire, and it is the young girl who nimbly walks across the rope. Ladies wander by, balancing huge trays of fruit on their heads, but dressed in the most colourful of outfits – there is never a dull moment.

Our evenings are spent in Madhu's, by now we are chatty with the young lad Ricky who was working here last year too. It looks like someone has bought him a replica Sunderland shirt as that seems to be his outfit of choice most nights, a little unfortunate for him! There is a good atmosphere about the place though; young children dressed up in Santa outfits, singing carols to earn a few tips before moving onto the next restaurant or bar to raise a few more rupees. It does make us smile at hearing these familiar Christmas tunes but sung with an Indian accent!

After repeating this routine for a few days, it is time for our trip to Hampi. Is it just us that is always in reception fifteen minutes before we are due to be picked up for any excursion? As usual the bus was ten minutes late... and then proceeded to head all the way out of Calangute down the Baga road picking up from various points before coming back past the roundabout right by the Mira – pretty sure we could have had an extra hour in bed if the pick-up route had been more favourable! With everyone aboard it was a very sleepy mini-bus that made its way to the train station in Vasco Da Gama. Our guide walks us through the station and onto the correct platform, hopefully us early risers have not disturbed the locals sleeping on the floor, and then just as dawn was breaking our train arrived.

It was our first experience aboard an Indian train and we were fortunate that our guide from the mini-bus was not shy in waking up passengers who were asleep in our seats. The train had been a sleeper train through the night, the back of the seat swings upwards and locks into place, providing an upper-level bunk. By this time of morning more passengers are booked on the train and that bed then becomes a seat once more, meaning the sleeping occupants must be disturbed. Luckily, there is no hard feelings, and within a minute or two of boarding we are trundling out of the station, on the way to Hospet for what is about a seven-hour journey.

While the seat was a bit short of padding, we thoroughly enjoyed our train journey, numb bottoms being the worst experience we had on our outbound leg. The views were fantastic, heading out past the Dudhsagar, a four-tiered waterfall located on the Mandovi River was one of the early highlights. Our westward journey continues, a smelly stop at Hubli station where the toilet is emptied and hosed down is one of the memories. Cups of chai and other snacks are available from sellers who board the train while it is stationary, by this stage we are both hungry and thirsty so take advantage of these human vending machines. I order two teas from one guy, but do not have the right money so off he goes; time passes and I have lost confidence that he is going to return, so with that I order another two from a different vendor who has the correct change... Typical, no sooner have we been passed our latest order when the first guy appears with our change and two more cups of chai! I should have had more faith...

The Western Ghats are rolling by on one side of the train whilst farmers are tending their land on the other side. No high-tech farm equipment here, oxen are providing the power for the ploughs in these parts. Local transport is on the back of a cart, suddenly, we are seeing a whole new side of India. Where the Golden Triangle had given us an insight into bustling cities and Goa demonstrates a tourist hot spot catering for international visitors, this is rural life. For mile after mile, you could imagine that these scenes have not changed for hundreds of years, or at least you can until you pass through a small town and see that every other shop is selling mobile phones... Just before we reach our destination station of Hospet, the mini-bus guide has a quiet word with us; when we get off at the station we are to wait, don't board the bus that all the others get on as we have separate transport. It transpires that everyone else has booked the Hampi trip through John's Boat Tours, we are the only clients of Valerie. At this stage we are not sure if this is good or bad news. Once all the others have boarded the coach our guide introduces us to a tuk-tuk driver, he will take us to our hotel, the Hampi International. This was all very plush, a very modern facility with a comfortable bed and soft duvet, two nights of good sleep beckons.

Having checked in and unpacked our minimal luggage we have the afternoon, or at least an hour or two before darkness to explore Hospet. The lady on reception points us in the direction of the 'town;' in reality it is just a transport hub, the closest place to Hampi on the railway line. Not deterred, we head out and it is good to stretch our legs after an entire day sitting down. We cross over the bridge and there are dozens of ladies doing their washing in the murky river, the washed clothes are then slapped around on the steps expelling all the excess water, before being bundled up to finish off drying at home. Pigs are wandering around eating at the rubbish, cows, not the regular Goan variety, but ones with massive horns were being driven through the streets, herds of them. This is one strange place.

With the light disappearing we head back home to freshen up. With no choice of restaurants in the town (we never really discovered anything), our only option is to eat at the hotel. The hotel restaurant is outside within the grounds of the hotel, open sided and with a nice feel about the place. We ordered a large Kingfisher beer between us when the waiter brought over the menus – and when he returns with the bottle, he presented it in the way a sommelier would the finest bottle of wine, cradled up his forearm like a proud father showing off his first new-born for us to look at before he opened it! Karnataka is a vegetarian state, so that meant our usual chicken options were off the menu; we need not have worried as the cashew nut curry was equally as delicious.

The best night's sleep we have had since arriving in Goa is followed up with a good breakfast before the bus picked us up for our day at Hampi. It seems like our co-passengers were not as happy with their accommodation, the food was poor, the rooms were tired - although the biggest complaint was reserved for the monkeys charging up and down the corridors... The ride to Hampi from Hospet is a short one, so our guide gives us a brief introduction on route, and of course we cannot remember much of it, but courtesy of a read of Wikipedia here is a brief, edited history ...

In the 14th century what we now know as Hampi was originally referred to as Vijayanagara, it was the capital of the Empire of the same name. At this time, it was an extremely prosperous and wealthy city – the richest in India by far. By the year 1500 it reached its height, and was the second largest medieval era city in the world, (only Beijing in China was larger at this time). Unfortunately, this peak was short lived and in 1565 the Vijayanagara Empire was defeated by a coalition of Muslim sultanates. At the battle of Talikota, King Aliya Rama Raya was betrayed by a pair of his army commanders, the Muslim Gilani brothers. What ought to have been an easy victory due to the sheer size of his army tuned into a crushing and an Empire ending defeat. With the city having been conquered, pillaged and destroyed by the sultanate armies the Kings head was separated from the rest of his body. The site then remained largely ignored until the mid-19th century. The current name of Hampi was taken from the name of a sacred inner suburb within the sprawling city.

In 1986 Hampi became a UNESCO world heritage site, and in total there are roughly sixteen hundred monuments and buildings remaining, covering an area of approximately sixteen square miles (a little over forty-one square km). Nearly all of the monuments were built between 1336 and 1570 CE during the Vijayanagara rule, many of them are still in amazing condition, allowing an insight into life here in those times.

So, in a nutshell we are looking at what was once one of the richest settlements in the world. Looking through our photographs this morning it is far better and bigger than we remember it. It does not have the one outstanding feature that makes something world famous, think the Taj Mahal, the Golden Temple or the Christ the Redeemer statue in Brazil. What it does have is a collection of monolith statues and a massive complex of fine buildings with beautiful carvings that are so crisp that they can still be made out perfectly. The landscape is stunning, huge great granite boulders defying gravity everywhere you look. What perhaps were old Temples clinging to the high rocky structures overlooking the Tungabhadra River, it really is difficult to compare it with anywhere else that we have ever visited. It is also very much still a living town; yes, it is on the tourist trail, and makes a good income from that, but at the same time there are people living here, local markets, guest houses, temples – it is very much like visiting a working museum. Our guide informs us that the guest houses in Hampi itself are for the Hindu and Jain visitors, for them it is an important pilgrimage site.

Our first point of call was the monolith statue of Ganesha, one of the largest statues of Lord Ganesha that exists in the southern part of India. The giant statue was carved out of a single huge boulder and is over fifteen-foot tall, it is set in a simple but beautiful stone structured Temple. The sleek granite pillars are decorated with various inscriptions and mythological characters, and with it being perched on a hill the views all around are equally breath-taking – hills and rolling countryside to one side and the abandoned city spread out before you on the other. Our tour guide gives us a brief insight to Ganesha, the story / myth of why he has the elephants head, snake belt etc. The pot-belly is supposed to be due to his fondness of sweets (his left hand is depicted holding them), but in our guides humorous explanation he explains that is what happens if you drink too much Kingfisher...

Next stop was the Virupaksha Temple, visible from miles around it is the main centre for pilgrims visiting Hampi, and had been considered the most sacred of places over the centuries. Dedicated to Lord Shiva It is remarkably intact among the surrounding ruins and is still used for worship today. While it is hard to draw your eyes away from the Temple itself you are now in what is the heart of Hampi. Outside of the gates is the market area and behind you, enclosed within the walls are lots of other ancient buildings that once made up this central complex.

The Temple itself is visually stunning; a nine storied stone construction, each layer being slightly smaller than the last, completely covered in carvings and topped off with a pair of cow horn shaped projections at the very top. If you are travelling with children then perhaps be ready to cover their eyes, the images of what they describe as 'erotic figures of the amorous couples' are hard-core porn! Such icons connected with fertility rites are considered auspicious on a philosophical ground, needless to say they caused a lot of smirking and sniggers followed by a closer inspection and a tilting of heads, to get a better angle by our tour group, average age of well over fifty! This temple is believed to date back to the seventh century, and have been in continuous use to this day – making it one of the oldest functioning temples in the whole of India. Over the centuries the temple gradually expanded into the sprawling spread of shrines and buildings that it has become today. The main entrance for this myriad of structures is through what is known as 'chariot street;' a tradition that is celebrated every February when they still have the annual chariot festival. In front of the main tower is the market area, often referred to these days as the Hampi Bazaar.

We visit the market before entering the gateway through to the rest of the town, its half aimed at the tourists but a lot of the stalls are also aimed at the local market, pots and pans, materials and everyday items that would not fit in your suitcase under the guise of a souvenir. It is a very colourful experience, flags passing overhead between the stalls that are set up on either side of the road. The usual bowls of coloured powders, exotic fruits and lady's saris make for a vivid colour palette. A snake charmer was doing well collecting tips and banana sales were going through the roof, by the size of his fruit mountain the stall holder was expecting to do a lot of trade. His assistant was pointing out the monkeys that were eyeing his stall from vantage points high up on the wall – no doubt it is the tourist's job to pay for their feed? Our guide catches up with us and says the Temple elephant is also fond of a banana or two, fortunately they are a lot cheaper than what Tesco's charge.

With the market done, fruit sourced and stored out of sight of the local primates we venture into the walled confines. A map is painted on one of the walls, no doubt helpful for anyone who has made the journey under their own steam to find their way from A to B. Within minutes of us being here the temple elephant enters the fray, you must hand it to the guides, they have a tight schedule but always get you in the right place at the right time. Queues of visitors feed the elephant a banana or two before it gently takes a rupee note from your hand and lays its trunk across your head as a form of blessing. I am not sure what denomination of note the elephant prefers, it did not seem fussy. The shrines around here are far better than what we expected, describing them as 'ruins' is unjust. The smell of spices and incense is pungent in the air, monkeys are watching you, the slightest sight of a yellow fruit and they will be down and help themselves to it.

The Narasimha statue at Hampi is a brilliant piece of sculpture, again cut from a single chunk of stone it is the biggest monolith in the area, standing at a staggering six point seven metres (twenty-two foot tall)! It is held in esteem as one of the finest existing samples of the Vijayanagar style of architecture. Can you imagine if the chisel had slipped near the end of the process and you had to start all over again... According to Hindu legend, Narasimha is the fourth incarnation of Vishnu and appeared on earth in the form of half human and half lion. In all honestly without being told that it would be difficult to recognise as that, the bulging eyes distract from everything else. Anyway, this monster of a sculpture sits there cross-legged, bare-chested, eyes-bulging and wearing what looks like a tall fez – or at least that was our interpretation of it. Rearing above its head is a canopy that represents the seven hoods of Adishesha, the king of all snakes. It is thought that the original sculpture included a small figure of the Goddess Lakshmi sitting on his lap, and even today the broken hand of the Goddess can be seen resting on the back of Narasimha.

Back aboard the bus and we only travel a short distance before we are offloaded again. We are now by some manicured gardens, and it is no surprise how immaculate they are, the lady is crouched down trimming them with shears the size of a big pair of scissors – hope she isn't on piecework? The Lotus Mahal was one of only a handful of buildings that had escaped damage when the empire was defeated, it is given that name because of the shape it resembles. The balcony and the passages are covered with a dome that looks like an opened lotus bud, and the central dome is also carved as a lotus bud. The palace is a two-storied building, well-proportioned symmetrically and very photogenic. Surrounded by a rectangular wall and four pyramid shaped towers the gardens are covered with many shady trees providing a cool peaceful aspect to the palace. The walls and pillars that support the arched windows and balcony of the palace are carved beautifully with patterns of mythical sea creatures and birds. The Lotus Mahal was designed as a palace for the royal ladies of those times to mingle around and enjoy recreational activities and musical concerts. These days one poor lady has the job of cutting the lawns with a pair of scissors in the midday heat...

The last stop before lunch was at the elephant stables, an image we were familiar with from the leaflets promoting this excursion. The elephant stable was constructed in the fifteenth century, during the reign of the Vijayanagara Empire; the attention to detail that has been put into the build shows the regard and importance afforded to the royal elephants of the time. The design is different to a lot of the buildings in Hampi, this is more in the Indo-Islamic style of architecture common across a lot of the country. The elephant stable is a long rectangular building made up of a row of eleven huge domed chambers. Each chamber is large enough to accommodate two elephants at a time and the entire length of the building is interconnected with internal arched openings. The central dome is the largest and most decorated of the eleven, its design is more in the architectural style found in the temples of Hampi. The other ten domes are more in the traditional Islamic style of architecture. The domes of the building were designed in a variety of shapes, such as, octagonal, circular, ribbed, drum-shaped and fluted, but all share that same symmetrical layout that we had just seen at the Lotus Mahal. In its day they would have been decorated with ornate plaster on the interior as well as the exterior. The elephant stable is another of the well-preserved buildings in Hampi, wear and tear has meant that the plaster has fallen off in some places, but considering it is more than six hundred years since it was constructed...

Following a fantastic lunch overlooking the river, rice and curries served up on a banana leaf at the Mango Tree restaurant (apparently, it's no longer there), we contemplated the next part of the tour. The coracles that we were to make our journey down river on did not look the safest floating things that we had ever seen, but they have been used on this river for centuries. We climb aboard this most ancient of transport, our guide is busy on his mobile phone and it is a young lad who gently propels us down the river until we reach our destination. It is a stunning setting, stone mountains towering above with mini acropolis type structures in places that look impossible to reach. The high-water mark is etched on the stones, far higher than its current level so it is hard to imagine that so much of what we are seeing could be covered by water at certain times of the year. The coracles were good fun, the only unsettling part was that when we were all getting aboard, they felt very unstable - once everyone was spread out, they were very steady, just not overly comfortable. Getting back up from sitting at floor level was not the easiest either!

The Kings Swing (or balance to give it its proper name) is something that we have seen in other places, in simplistic terms the fatter the King meant more goodies for his subjects – which stretched to gold here in Hampi! Still near the banks of the river and we visit the Vittala Temple, perhaps the grandest and most photographed in Hampi. The temple exemplifies the immense creativity and architectural excellence possessed by the sculptors and artisans of this era. This temple complex is in a sprawling area, with many halls, shrines and pavilions within the high compound walls accessed by three towering gateways.

It is within these walls that the most symbolic image of Hampi resides, the Stone Chariot. The chariot stands in the courtyard of the temple, and is one of the three most famous stone chariots in the whole of India, more importantly it is considered to be the most stunning piece of architecture in the whole of the Vijayanagara kingdom. It is actually a shrine that has been designed in the shape of an ornamental chariot and dedicated to Garuda (Garuda is the carrier of Lord Vishnu). We are told that there is even an image of Garuda enshrined into the sanctum, but for that we will have to take his word for it. The wheels of the chariot were once functional, or at least they could be rotated – but these days they have been fixed to prevent any further damage to them.

Within a stone's throw is the Ranga Mantapa, famous for its 56 musical pillars. These musical pillars are also known as SAREGAMA pillars, indicating the musical notes emitted by them. Now I interpret that as the Indian version of DO, RE, MI, FA and the scales from the Sound of Music. When played, no doubt by someone who knows what they are doing, the musical notes can be made out when the pillars are tapped gently. These musical pillars do not just provide entertainment, they also have the important job of holding up the roof. Amazingly these musical pillars inside the Vittala Temple complex were each carved out of huge single pieces of resonant stone. Each main pillar is surrounded by seven minor pillars and it is these seven minor pillars that each produces a different musical note, are you with me so far? The notes emerging from these pillars vary in sound quality depending on whether the instrument is a percussion, string or wind instrument. I hope that makes sense as it was very impressive both to look at and hear, but these days even tapping the musical pillars to emit musical notes is a big no-no. If you have not visited you will have to take my word for it. Our guide describes it to us as a nightclub of its day, it is a place of music where you do not even need to bring any instruments!

An interesting fact; the British rulers of India were so puzzled by these musical pillars that they cut two of them in half to check whether anything existed inside aiding the emission of musical notes. Nothing was found and the two pillars cut by the British rulers still

*exist inside the temple complex and can be seen by
visitors even today – I guess you just need to know
whereabouts they are.*

The road leading to this temple group is in a sorry state. Once the location of a thriving market known as the Vittala Bazaar it was famous for horse trading, and the ruins of the market can still be seen on either side of the road today - there are even carvings inside the temple that represent images of foreigners trading horses. It is hard to imagine what this place would have been like when it was a thriving city. So far today we had visited temples and statues, rode in a coracle down the river, eaten lunch off a banana leaf, what we were to see next was what left the biggest impression on me, a feat of engineering that was both practical and stunning to look at – the water tanks and aqueducts. If only Akbar had learned from here, Fatehpur Sikri could all have ended so differently.

The water tanks, or what they called pushkaranis, are scattered right across the site of Hampi and display great architectural beauty. Nothing was made ugly by these craftsmen! The tanks related to the temples were considered sacred and used to supply water for the ritualistic purposes of those temples. The one situated within the Royal Enclosure would have been built for the royal family of Vijayanagara and fed the prodigious baths that can still be seen. These look majestic; it is not just the beautiful carvings and pillars that remain but also some of the largest ornamental stone taps that you are likely to see. Do not think baths like in your home, these have more in common with swimming pools; from the doorways are steps that take you down perhaps four-foot, the taps are five-foot high and protrude from the wall by a foot or so. The bath slash swimming pool is bigger than a tennis or squash court, so it would have been very much a communal event. Everything here is done on an excessive scale but with an artistic eye, finesse and attention to detail.

Trying to describe the water tanks is difficult, it is like a giant sunken square, an upside-down four-sided pyramid, that you step down into. This one here is a five-tiered tank with each tier comprising of a few steps. The next tier down would be slightly smaller than the previous and so on – the clever part of this design is that the water level was irrelevant, whether full or near empty, access would be easy for everyone. Symmetrical... that word again, you could hold a mirror across the centre and see the whole thing as intended from its reflection. The water was fed into the tanks from the Tungabhadra River and then fed all around the local area by an extensive network of stone aqueducts and canals. Surprisingly, some of these water channels are functional even today. The water tank we are looking at looks in pristine condition, or at least to our untrained eyes! Not in such good shape is the colonnade surrounding it, and the decorative columns that we are being told about have long since gone...

As we wander back towards the bus our guide is earning his tips right until the end. On the walls are fish symbols, and he tells us that these were used to point the way to the water tanks. By this stage we are a weary bunch, it has been a long hot day and we are going to finish it off with a final mini-bus ride to a viewing point to watch the sunset... Predictably, and we often are unlucky weather wise, the early evening cloud had come down so we didn't get the full glorious effect. With dusk having reached there was nothing else to do but return to the hotel and the Kingfisher sommelier...

We were fortunate that the train journey in both directions just flew by. On the outbound journey the carriage was full of younger European backpackers who had plenty of (horror?) stories to pass on of their travels through India; nightmare journeys involving cramped, overcrowded trains and bus crashes – despite all of that they were loving every minute of the experience. Returning to Goa we were surrounded by a large group of young Indian agricultural students who were all keen to practise their (already very good) English on us. What was good to see (and hear), is how clued up they were about Indias issues with litter; while many older Indians on the trains threw their rubbish straight out the window they were as annoyed by that as us. Maybe the next generation might make for a cleaner country?

Back in Goa we took a fishing trip from Sinquerim, this would be my first ever taste of fishing with a rod – what a place to start! As a child I had been crabbing in Wells and used a fishing net on a stick around rock pools when on holiday. Alison had far more experience, holidays on the Norfolk Broads, fishing from a boat made her semi-professional in my eyes. It was a short drive to the jetty and then a very pleasant boat ride out around the peninsula, the old jail looking down upon us from the cliff top. The guy on the boat provided us with bait, would it be fair to lay blame there? Over the next two hours all my dreams involving a huge catch, that photograph where I was struggling to hold a fish of such size came crashing down – I never caught a thing. Alison using her vast experience caught two, the first one was small and thrown back in, the second one was big enough for the boat owner to take home for his tea...

Walking the streets of Calangute one day we also see an elephant wandering the streets. Well, when I say wandering, I mean being led by a tall bearded guy wearing bright orange robes. The elephant itself had a colourful chalk design on its face and upper trunk with its ears sporting a heart design! Sat aboard was a second guy - not on the neck of the animal like the mahouts at Jaipur but on a huge cushioned throw on its back. Visitors were having their pictures taken with the huge beast, and then the chap in the orange robes would be looking for tips, bringing out his book with how much other people had donated to the local temple. Chatting to others, years ago this was a regular sight but it was the only time that we ever encountered this spectacle, it certainly knocks the donkeys at Skegness into a cocked hat!

Before we knew it our time in Goa was over. Having spoken to Valerie we already knew where our next out of state excursion would be to, and on our return home we also discovered the real reason Lauren had changed her mind coming with us. The old lady next door was chatting to us about our holiday and then asked us how long Lauren had been seeing her boyfriend for? "What boyfriend?" was our question... She had got a better option than a trip to Goa, an empty house for two weeks.

If we weren't overly impressed with our daughter, here is what we thought of the Mira Hotel...

Great location if a little noisy

Review of Mira Hotel

We had been this hotel before when it had a fantastic Thai restaurant attached, unfortunately that is no longer there. The hotel is in a great location, but that does bring a noise problem (dogs, crows, car horns etc) so pack some earplugs. The rooms are adequate but cleaned regular & the bathroom is one big wet room & again more than adequate. The pool is a good size but unfortunately most the sun beds are in the shade for the entire day. Breakfast was the basic tea & toast & although there was a menu card for additional breakfast items, lunches & dinners I don't think we ever see anyone eat at the hotel. We will be booking again next year as it is perfectly located within 10 minutes of out 3 favourite restaurants.

November 2012 - Goa, Rajasthan and Mumbai

We made a bad decision this year. The three-hour drive home from Gatwick airport to Lincolnshire was always a nightmare, so for a change we chose to take the Manchester flight. It is still roughly the same drive time - but a change is as good as a rest. We would also book a hotel and parking package, travel down the day before our flight and enjoy getting up knowing the airport was close by. Little did we know...

We had already had an inconvenient flight change through from SpiceJet that had meant adding a stay in Mumbai onto our itinerary, our original plans had just been to visit Udaipur and Jodhpur in Rajasthan. A change to scheduling by SpiceJet meant that our flights arrival from Jodhpur into Mumbai was now ten minutes after our flight from Mumbai to Goa had departed! In simple terms our connecting flights just did not connect! A desperate phone call to Valerie and all was sorted, why not spend the best part of twenty-four hours in Mumbai and catch the next day's flight back to Goa? That made sense to us, an opportunity to see the sights of an extra Indian city without any additional flight costs involved, just the expense of one night's accommodation, we would already be there. Problem solved.

All had gone so well in getting to our hotel close to Manchester airport, we had enjoyed a pub lunch on route, all relaxed and civilised compared to our usual schlepp down to Gatwick. We had a good night's sleep, no concerns about traffic problems, no need to allow time for breakdowns, we were already there, or within touching distance. The fun began next morning when we arrived at the airport; as usual we were early, so no queues at our check-in. As usual we had beaten the rush, time to offload our cases and then we can relax, the holiday starts from now ... Rather than us hand over our cases the lady at check-in hands us a sheet of paper. It is not good news.

Before long, the rest of our fellow passengers for the flight that is going nowhere fast had arrived, and then we were given the news that everyone had feared. We were spending another night in a Manchester airport hotel; food vouchers were handed out and we would be given more information as they had it. Overall, we were delayed for around thirty hours before we finally took off much to the relief of all. Our biggest problem was that with such a long delay we were due to fly back out of Goa the day after we had arrived!

For the second year running we had booked into the Hotel Mira, this time we had emailed ahead and asked for one of the rooms by the pool block – they would so much quieter than the ones facing the road. It was good to be back, and the room was great – from our doorstep an Olympic long jumper could easily leap into the swimming pool. First stop for us though was a trip to Valerie Travels, we still had the balance to pay for our trip departing tomorrow. It was a strange day; we didn't get down to the beach at all – the usual first meal was at Mirabai's and a couple of afternoon beers in Madhu's, where by now we are recognised by the lads who own it and receive a warm welcome. It is back to our room to sort out our luggage, a small cabin bag each will suffice with some ruthless planning.

Our flight to Udaipur was split in two with a change in Mumbai, the first leg was a standard jet plane but the second part was by a propellor driven one. It seemed so small in comparison, just the two seats either side of the aisle and the stairs aboard were part of the plane that folded outwards and down to the ground! We need not have worried, we arrived safe and well, where we were picked up from the airport and taken the short journey to our guest house nestled on the lake.

The two guest houses we booked for this excursion were more basic than what Valerie wanted to book us into, in her defence she tends to use what are higher end, more westernised style hotels, that way European tourists are well within their comfort zones. We wanted to experience a more authentic family run place; if it is clean, we are more than happy, regardless of how basic the amenities. Our accommodation in Udaipur was a lovely little place called Sargam Sadan, right on the shores of Lake Pichola. Everything about it was perfect, gracious hosts, comfortable room and delicious food. What it had for us was an abundance of charm, it was decorated traditionally and we felt like it represented where you were in the world. The restaurant on the top floor, offered standard tables and seating to suit westerners but also cushions on a raised bed where you could sit cross-legged with a small bench table for locals. The views from this top floor were stunning, looking right across the lake to the mountains beyond. Tomorrow we would be picked up after breakfast to explore this city and its palaces further.

Udaipur is a breath of fresh air as Indian cities go, no wonder it was called the most romantic spot on the continent of India by British administrator James Tod in or around the year 1800. It has not been short of platitudes since, often referred to as the Venice of the

East or the city of lakes, and in 2009 Udaipur was voted the Best City in the World by the Travel + Leisure magazine. With such a title there is no wonder that tourism is big business here - The Taj Lake Palace and the Leela Palace are amongst the most expensive hotels in the country, but neither can match The Oberoi Udaivilas, which was ranked as the world's number 1 hotel in 2015. I can quickly confirm that the Sargam Sadan was not in that price category, yet it does share the same lakeside location, amazing views and convenience for the city sights.

The views that I have just mentioned have also been featured on our TV screens and cinemas. The 1983 James Bond film Octopussy features both the lake and the city itself, the 1980's mini-series The Jewel in the Crown and more recently The Best Exotic Marigold Hotel have all brought the cameras and clapper boards to the city. The list does go on, but with not being a film buff myself, most of them went over my head! If you are into your Bollywood films then the list of films that feature the sights of Udaipur is as long as your arm.

Our guide picks us up on time and our first stop is just a short drive away, the Jagdish Temple. It is a large Hindu temple very close to the Royal Palace and has been a place of continuous worship since the mid seventeenth century. Dedicated to Vishnu the Jagdish temple was earlier known as the temple of Jagannath Rai, one of the thousand(!) names of the Hindu God Vishnu. The Jagdish temple represents one of the best architectural wonders of the Mewar dynasty, and is built in keeping the rules of Vastushastra, the Hindu architectural science in mind. Set upon a raised platform, flaunting intricately carved pillars that lead you into its airy halls with painted walls, all adorned with vibrant colours and lavishly decorated ceilings. Two massive elephant statues of stone welcome visitors to this ancient building. By the statues is an inscription engraved on the stone slab celebrating Mahara Jagat Singh who ordered the construction of the temple. Standing twenty-four metres (seventy-nine feet) high, the summit of the main temple is further decorated with carvings of horsemen, elephants, musicians and dancers who are said to have practiced here during the time when the temple was being established. A brass image of Garuda, half man, and half eagle guards the gates before you find the main shrine and a four-armed image of Lord Vishu himself. It is believed that the statue of Lord Vishnu tends to have a hypnotic effect on the devotees and bring a sense of calmness and serenity, something that Udaipur has by the bucketful.

It was the nearby City Palace that would be our next stop, why we needed to get back in the car just to cross the street and head round the corner remains a mystery! As soon as we approached the palace, we could see that it was a hive of activity – in the grounds and courtyard were tables being set up for a lavish wedding ceremony. Udaipur is famous for its weddings; you haven't made it in either Bollywood or business if you do not get married here, and no doubt your available budget is used to rank what rung you are at on the ladder of success. The flower sculptures that were being carefully arranged would take days to complete going by the size of the framework that they were working on, without doubt there is big money spent and big money to be made in the extravagant world of Indian weddings.

What also becomes clear is that this tour is going to be a light affair, it is more about taking in the sights than the facts that sometimes leave us wallowing amongst dates and names from history. That does not mean we escaped that completely... The City Palace was built over a period of nearly four hundred years, with contributions across that time from several rulers of the Mewar dynasty. The first stone was laid in 1553 by Maharana Udai Singh II of the Sisodia Rajput family as he looked to create his own city rather than continuing to rule from Chittor. The palace is located on the east bank of Lake Pichola and has several other palaces within the region, two of them can be seen from here. Where other palaces were often built within bigger structures, usually forts, this flamboyant assembly is considered the largest of its type in the state of Rajasthan. Built on top of a hill, in a fusion of the Rajasthani Rajput architecture it provides panoramic views of the city and the surrounding mountains. It has the perfect vantage point, overlooking not just Lake Pichola but also several other historic monuments like the Lake Palace, Jag Mandir, the Jagdish Temple and the Monsoon Palace - the views are something else. Interestingly only Jag Mandir is older than the City Palace, it was started a couple of years earlier in 1551.

The Mewar kingdom was established in the year 568 AD by Guhil, the first Maharana of Mewar. By the eighth century the capital was based in Chittor, a hilltop fort from where the Sisodia's ruled for eight hundred years. Maharana

Udai Singh II inherited the Mewar kingdom at Chittor in 1537 but by that time their power was already in decline due to the constant wars with the Mughal empire. Udai Singh II relocated to the site near Lake Pichola for his new kingdom as the location was well protected on all sides by forests, lakes and the Aravalli hills. Constant factions left the Mewar state in dire straits until in 1818, Maharana Bhim Singh signed a treaty with the British - accepting their protection against the other feuding empires. After the Indian independence in 1947, the Mewar Kingdom, (along with other princely states of Rajasthan), merged with the democratic India. The Mewar Kings lost their special royal privileges and titles, but did retain their ownership of the palaces in Udaipur and converted parts of the palace complex into heritage hotels.

The Palace facade overlooking Lake Pichola runs for nearly two hundred and fifty metres (eight hundred feet) in length, and is just over thirty metres (one hundred foot) in height. Overseeing the four hundred years of building were twenty-two different Maharana's, so it is no surprise that there is a collection of structures, including eleven small separate palaces. The unique aspect of this medley of buildings is that the architectural design is distinctly similar, so the finished article is pleasing on the eye. Being built entirely in granite and marble avoids conflicts of design to an extent, there is no obvious sign of where one era of building started and the previous ended. A pair of the eleven palaces mentioned have since been turned into heritage hotels, and to complement them the complex has incorporated additional facilities catering for the needs of high-end tourists - a post office, bank, travel agency, craft shops and even an Indian boutique belonging to the World Wildlife Fund (WWF). The entire complex remains as the property of the Mewar royal family with various trusts responsible for maintaining the structures and securing their future.

On our tour of the Golden Triangle, it was the buildings within the forts at Jaipur and Agra that were the stars of the show. From the outside they were set in vast sandstone structures, but from the inside they were full of finesse and delicate carvings. Here is very much the opposite, inside there is not much open to the public, even less than normal today with them preparing for a wedding. The exterior and the views is what this building is all about, and what better way to see them than a boat trip on Lake Pichola taking in Jag Mandir at the same time?

From our boat we travel the length of the City Palace and its gardens, it absolutely towers above us, all domes and thick solid walls with the odd tree overhanging the lake. The true beauty of the palace is better seen from a distance, and to fit it in a photograph it needs to be a good distance away.

From our boat our guide points out that we can see three palaces, the Monsoon Palace is visible up in the hills, the City Palace in all its glory and the Lake Palace rising from the waters to the right of us. Whilst the Lake Palace was originally built for use in the height of summer, it is now a luxury five-star hotel, operating under the Taj Hotels Resorts and Palaces banner. The design is impressive, the whole structure has been built over an existing island from shining white marble and appears just to be rising majestically from the water, all sign of the outcrop of land it is perched upon has cleverly been hidden.

Jag Mandir, or the Lake Garden Palace as it is sometimes called is situated on another natural island at the southern end of Lake Pichola. The man-made lake was initially created in the fifteenth century by a local Banjara tribal chieftain for carrying grain across the streams. In 1560, the lake was enlarged substantially by constructing dams across two streams creating what we see today. It takes its name Jag Mandir from the main palace, which also incorporates the Gul Mahal, the Gul Mahal was the very first structure that was built. The corner towers of the palace are octagonal in shape, topped with cupolas. Inside a labyrinth of reception halls, residential suites and internal courts were built, all in traditional Rajput and Mughal architectural styles.

Like the City Palace, the best view of here is from the approach, the landing jetty or the entry pavilion to give it its proper title is decorated with large elephants carved in stone, four on each side of the entrance steps. The trunks of these elephants were damaged over the years and have since been replaced with... polystyrene! The flower garden, which gives it that alternative name is set up in the large Garden Courtyard, itself simply decorated with black and white tiles. The plant life brings a colourful addition to the white stone that you see everywhere else, yew bushes, frangipani trees, bright bougainvillea and jasmine plants. Palm trees add height whilst fountains and water pools, crisscrossed by walkways with low marble handrails, bedeck the garden surroundings. We are told that we are fortunate to have access to the courtyard as the present Maharana uses this part of the Jag Mandir to host lavish parties himself.

A boat journey back to the Bansi Ghat jetty and the short walk back to the car, more gardens are our next stop. Small but perfectly formed, is the best way to describe these... Saheliyon-ki-Bari, or Garden of the Maidens has fountains and kiosks, a lotus pool and marble elephants. Legend has it that the garden was designed by Maharana Sangram Singh as a wedding gift for his queen. The queen was accompanied by forty-eight maids in her marriage, and these gardens provided them with pleasurable moments away from the royal court. Another Maharana, Bhopal Singh, also loved this place and built an additional pavilion of rain fountains. These fountains were imported from England, and are in the form of sculpted birds that spurts water from their beaks producing the rain effect.

And with that ended our tour of the highlights of Udaipur. It had been an enjoyable day, shorter than some that we have had in the past, but in a good way – on the odd occasion we have had more than enough before the days tour is complete! We had thoroughly enjoyed the boat trip and the fresh clean air that is not always associated with India, the balance of the tour was good too, nothing too heavy but at the same time we had learned a lot. With a couple of hours of daylight left this afternoon, and a whole morning to ourselves tomorrow we felt, for the very first time, here is an Indian city that we can find our way around, explore and relax in...

After being dropped back at the Sargam Sadan it was a quick freshen up before we ventured back out, only this time under our own steam. From our lakeside location it was a short walk up to the main road and a right turn, back towards the city gates, the bridges and the temples. In the square just before the main road was a mosque and outside of that was a water pump, maybe there is no mains water connected to everywhere around here as it was being used by a stream of locals filling up containers. School had obviously finished for the day as there was streams of school children heading home for the day, smiling and waving at us. Like in Goa, late afternoon is the time of day to start frying snacks, we watched for ten minutes or so as some guy had a pan of oil heating on the floor outside his shop, cooking all types of delights. Suddenly the street was full of donkeys, or at least that is what they looked like to us. Each of them was covered with a sack cloth over their backs and what looked like a slightly padded seat, they weren't being ridden but more herded through the streets by a group of ladies. Our walk was not taking us far, there was so much going on that we spent more time stopped watching than walking. With the sun beginning to dip behind the buildings we head back, tomorrow morning we would try again – now was the time for a seat on the rooftop with a cold beer in hand, watching the lights come on around the lake as darkness falls.

The next morning, we head out again, determined that today we will find our way to the city gates. In no time we have covered further than our short walk took us yesterday, we had been too distracted by all the activity from the shops, and the donkeys – nothing is ever dull in India! Beyond the shops the lake reappears to our right, and it looks like it is wash day. The washing part has already been done; the white sheets are now laid out on the sandy shores of the lake drying... now I am no laundry expert, but to me that does not seem ideal as I imagine them looking dirtier than before they were washed. The gates of the city are by now within sight, leading up to them is a long wall running alongside the lake, strangely it is topped with substantial numbers of cow (or buffalo) poo patties... We are looking at them puzzled, trying to work out what they are for when some stranger explains to us that they are used for cooking on, once dried out they burn very well and Wikipedia even knows how much energy in kilojoules, 'One dung cake of an average size gives 2100 kJ worth of energy'. I am unsure if they were of average size though, as have never seen them before, but I would describe these as having a seven- or eight-inch diameter, and being about the thickness of a good burger.

As we approach the gates we are walking along a bridge, the lake flowing under the road at this point and around the outside of the city walls – and for some reason the cows seem to congregate here. Maybe it's the clock-in for the dung cake factory? Stepping around them and we cannot help but notice the huge great spikes that are on the city gates, something that had passed us by when we drove through them only yesterday. It is safe to say that these towering gates never close, but in the days when they did these spikes would have been big enough to have stopped even the charge of an elephant, they seem set at that sort of height, about eight foot above the ground, no danger to your average pedestrian just walking by. That is the benefit of being on foot, the slower pace allows you to pick up details that you would otherwise miss.

Once inside the city walls, we can see the Jagdish Temple, so we walk as far as that and just sit and watch for a little while. With one eye on the time, we set off on a leisurely walk back home, a driver is picking us up around midday for our onwards journey to Jodhpur, with a visit to the Jain temple at Ranakpur on route. Alison is keen to look in some of the local shops selling scarves in every colour under the sun, souvenirs for both our Mum's. Shops here are so different to what we expected, we have got used to the Goa style of selling; here there is no hard sell, no ridiculous starting price with you knowing that you need to get down to half of what you are being asked for! By the time we leave the shop we have bought more scarves than we intended, they were at such a fair price and of such excellent quality that rather than narrow it down to three we ended up with five.

Having said our goodbyes at the Sargam Sadan we were back on the road, and after just over two hours travel, we reach the Chaturmukha Dharana Vihara Temple - more commonly just referred to as the Jain Temple of

Ranakpur. We seemed to have been in touching distance of here for a long while, the last ten miles or so seemed to take forever, the road winding upwards in ever tighter curves until we finally arrived. Visually wise it is a feast for the eyes, a grand white marble structure with twenty-nine halls, eighty domes, 1,444 marble pillars and 426 columns. As if that is not enough the backdrop is one of trees and greenery, nothing else in sight apart from this one perfectly white temple rising majestically from the slope of a hill.

The construction was started in the first half of the fifteenth century, and is said to have been inspired by a divine vision of a Jain businessman, Darna Shah. Many sculptors and artists submitted their designs to Shah but none of them matched the image he had dreamt of, or at least that was the case until an architect named Deepak from Mundara arrived. Deepak proposed a design that matched up to Shah's own vision so he sought the land to build the temple from King Rana Kumbha. Not only did the king give a substantial piece of land to build the temple on, he was so impressed by the plans himself that he also asked Deepak to build a town around it. The build of the temple alone took fifty years and nearly three thousand men, and the name of both the town and temple are taken from Rana Kumbha, who was the ruler of Mewar at the time but also fully supportive of the dream had by Darna Shah. The Ranakpur temple is one of the largest and most important temples of Jain culture.

Jain temples are well known for their sculptural work, but this temple is famous for having the most intricate carvings and unique architecture of them all. The 1,444 marble pillars, each carved individually and with exquisite detail are all different, no two pillars are the same. There are several myths about this temple, some say that it is impossible to count all the pillars, whilst another relates to why one pillar has been left incomplete. Some say this was to stop the place from being perfect, others say that every time that pillar was built it had fallen again by the next morning. Supposedly there are also eighty-four underground chambers built to protect the Jain idols from the Mughals.

Carving wise we have never seen anything like it, how can it even be possible to produce 1444 unique designs for all these pillars? Is it possible to count them all, it would be if you were to put a mark on each one to avoid counting it twice, but somehow, I do not think that would go down to well! It is not like the carving ends at the pillars, the door frames are incredible and as for the biggest dome of the ceiling... it is impossible to describe the work and hours that must have gone into that. While we have seen many incredible places the sheer creativity of here takes some beating, all the decorative touches are done solely through carvings in sparkling, polished white marble. There is nothing else on the colour palette, no glass and mirrors, just awesome carvings wherever you look – where else could you turn and see engraved nymphs playing the flute in various dance postures fifty foot in the air? Once again it has been a place that we have never heard of that has completely blown us away and exceeded all our expectations. I have since discovered, while researching this piece, that the Ranakpur Temple had made it onto the final seventy-seven strong shortlist of wonders, from which the new Seven Wonders of the World were chosen (2007). It is completely worthy of a place on that list, one of the most stunning buildings that we have ever seen for sure.

It is a further three hours plus drive before we reach the blue city of Jodhpur, and our next accommodation at the Kiran Vilas. This place was more along the lines of a home stay rather than a hotel, but what an experience! The family run the place from top to bottom, and as well as big spacious rooms there are the gardens / courtyard to enjoy a beer or two in. They also run a restaurant next door so you can even eat there as well if you like. Throughout our stay here though we never had a key, the owner told us that the previous occupant had forgot to hand in on their departure and he could not find a spare. We were not too worried as the room was part of the family home, the art hanging on the walls and the artifacts and ceremonial swords that adorned the grand furniture in the corridors looked far more valuable than anything we were leaving behind in the room.

With darkness having already fell we ate at the restaurant, albeit sat in the courtyard of our accommodation. In all honesty the food was not up to much, gristly and bland – or at least too our taste, hopefully tomorrow we would have our bearings and eat elsewhere. After our meal we were sat having another beer when an elderly guy came and asked if he could join us, introducing himself as the owner of the Kiran Vilas. Once he had introduced himself, we recognised him from some of the photographs on the walls in reception, what he did we never found out, but in the numerous framed pictures he was always shaking hands at some ceremony or other – we can only assume he was an important person in these parts. VIP or not though, he was a lovely friendly guy and by the time we went to bed he had bought us a couple more beers and was planning to cook his special goat curry for us tomorrow evening!

Following a good traditional Indian breakfast, we were picked up by our tour guide and taken into Jodhpur, first stop the imposing Mehrangarh Fort. Unlike the Amber Fort at Jaipur there is nothing fairy-tale like about its appearance, this is a huge, square and impenetrable looking fort sat on a rocky hill top. It was originally constructed in 1459 by Rajput ruler Rao Jodha, though most of what can be seen today is from the seventeenth century. Apart from the one road snaking its way down to the city below it seems inaccessible and unwelcoming. This colossus of a building (maybe) gets its name from Mehr meaning the Sun, and Garh, which means fort - the Rathore dynasty worshipped the Sun god, so a very apt name that sounds feasible. The crop of rock that it sits astride is called Bhakur Cheeria which translates as 'The Mountain of Birds.' Stories and myths about this place run rife - from the one about four people that were buried alive, one in each corner of the fort, through to the name in fact coming from 'Mehran' a local man, who was sacrificed by being thrown alive from the hilltop. Separating fact from fiction is nigh on impossible, in fact the more you search the more stories and the muddier the water gets!

If the outside of the fort just screams brutal, inside is a complete surprise – fine carvings, delicate touches at every turn and lots of pictures of Maharajas with big moustaches. Our first stop is at the museum within the fort where there are collections of turbans amongst the exhibits, documenting changes of style through the years but also examples of ceremonial headwear. Of course, the armoury collection features strongly but with such juxtaposition it sits by some of the finest miniature paintings from the Marwar dynasty. Transport also featured strongly in the museum, none of it with wheels but of various methods of being carried around. One of the sedans was beautifully domed and exquisitely decorated, the long handles either side carved with lions. Others were made to perch upon top of an elephant, some more luxurious than others. One looks like it could have been taken from a roller coaster at Alton Towers, only the lion with its raised foot and the accompanying parasol wouldn't have been very streamlined. Reading up more, these two seaters were called howdahs; covered with gold and silver embossed sheets, the front compartment, (with more leg space) was meant for the King or royalty, with the rear smaller one for a trusted bodyguard disguised as an attendant.

Another fort and another Sheesh Mahal, a palace of glass and mirrors – say it quietly, but this could be the best one yet! Others seemed to have added a touch of blue, here they have not held back - with blue, green, orange, silver and gold ornaments dangling from the ceiling... This is a real assault on your eyes; it is another magnificent structure, covered in elaborate mirror work from floor to ceiling. Brightly coloured murals of religious characters compliment the twinkling, reflecting light that is cascading throughout the room. Interestingly, the Sheesh Mahal was Maharaja Ajit Singh's bedchamber during his reign as Maharaja of Jodhpur from 1679 to 1724 – however did he get to sleep?

The courtyards are so ornate, decked out with cornices, columns and domes. Lattice work covers the hundreds of openings, providing for both shade and cooling breezes in equal measures. As usual the tour guide has his favourite spots, us peering from a balcony, photographs taken through the latticework providing an arty touch. The most mesmerising part of this fort is not within the buildings though, it is the view when you look out over the city of Jodhpur. From this vantage point you can see exactly why it is called the blue city. Driving through the city it was not so noticeable, yet with this bird's eye view from above it is an incredible sight – and very blue...

And why is jodhpur painted blue, or at least the homes in the old town? Once more it is difficult to find the exact reason, we are told by our guide that it all comes down to the caste system and social status. Blue is firmly linked as the colour of the Brahmin community, a high caste within India and they use the colour to distinguish themselves from lower castes, hence painting their homes and businesses in blue. Brahmins are associated with priests and religious teachings and with that are recognised as the highest of the four social castes. Other, equally plausible explanations, are that it is done to help deter termites. The blue paint is a mixture of copper sulphate and limestone that not only wards off bugs, but also creates a calming effect. Further backing up this argument is that there are many other castes than just Brahmins living in the blue-painted houses. Is it to keep the houses cool? Blue is a good reflector of heat, and when temperatures regularly hit forty degrees and more any help is appreciated. Take your pick of those, or even the more fanciful legend... the colour blue is associated with Lord Shiva, and during the time of Samudra Manthan he drank a poison to save the planet. The effects of the toxic liquid turned his body blue, and from that day forward his followers considered it to be a sacred colour...

Having finished our tour of the fort we wind our way back to the foot of the hill and visit Ghanta Ghar and the Sardar market that is wrapped all around it. Ghanta Ghar is the name of the famous clock tower that was built by Sardar Singh in the late eighteenth century, and that is who the market takes its name from. The clock tower is pleasant enough, but I think we are here more for the views of the fort towering over this old part of the city. Never the less we are happy to wander around the market and see what is going on. Set in a perfect square, it is surrounded on all sides by a row of shops with arched verandas. It is another one of those places that would have been flawless in its simplicity and symmetry, but over the years additional builds and extensions now detract from the grand design. Maybe we are just over a hundred years too late to see it at its finest? We strolled through and around, enjoying the shop keepers displays, fruit and vegetables mixed in with a shop selling slippers, not like we have at home but ones with curled up toes like in Ali Baba and the Forty Thieves.

This is very much still a picturesque square, with local colour and merchandise mixed in with your usual Indian randomness. Squalor, rubbish swept into piles ready for the wandering cows next meal. Hairdressers, or at least a man sat on the floor being shaved with a glinting cut-throat razor. Abandoned, or randomly parked scooters, carts that must have been in use long before the clock tower was even built are still in use, yoked up to oxen. The familiar sight of dogs sleeping alongside the lesser-spotted highly decorated camel that is wearing a mesh string covered in pom-poms of all colours... Colourful and chaotic, there is something for everyone here, locals and tourists alike – again, all remarkably hassle free, we plan to return under our own steam.

There is nothing quite like visiting cremation grounds when you are on holiday! Our next stop is at the Jaswant Thada, a memorial in polished marble that is sometimes described as the 'Taj Mahal of Marwar.' It was built in memory of Maharaja Jaswant Singhjill by his son Maharaja Sardar Singhji and completed in 1906. We park up by the lake and climb the steep red sandstone steps until we reach the white marble of the memorial. More steps, this time in white marble to reach a further level with a red sandstone balustrade, before finally we enter the building. Inside it is a nice blend of the white marble with a little black trim, but the reality is it is another one of those 'zebra' moments. Yes, an attractive enough building, but in the scheme of what we have already seen... If we are not overly enamoured by the building then the gardens and cenotaphs sitting astride the massive boulders have us won over. The views across the lake and over to the Mehrangarh fort are not too shabby either.

Today's ultimate destination is the Umaid Bhawan Palace Hotel, somewhere that is well out of our price range! It was built between 1929 and 1943 and was the main residence of the former Jodhpur royal family. Interestingly the reason behind the Umaid Bhawan being built, one of the biggest royal buildings in the world, was to create employment for the local farmers. At the time of construction, Jodhpur was experiencing drought and hardship, this project would aid the locals, helping them to earn a good living. With the build taking so long Umaid Singh, who was behind the clever plan, lived in the palace for a little more than four years before he died in 1947. Hanwant

Singh, who succeeded him, also died at an early age when the plane he was returning home in crashed just five years later.

These days the 347-room palace is divided into three parts, some remain as the residence of the royal family, part is now part of the luxury Taj Palace Hotel and the remainder houses a museum focusing on the twentieth century history of the Jodhpur Royal Family. Whilst we don't go into the museum, we are able to see the collection of luxury cars that are housed here as part of the collection. As for a night at the hotel, a quick visit on Google suggests that you are looking at a minimum of six hundred pound per night, that is for a budget room, but to be fair it does look tastefully decorated...

Our day is done, or at least our organised tour part is. Safely delivered back to the Kiran Vilas we have a quick freshen up before venturing back out. We set off on foot, and find time for a cup of chai at a street vendor, who, in no time has dusted down a pair of industrial sized paint pots, we have just been given the best seats in the house! Watered, we continue on our way, not exactly certain that we are even heading in the right direction. In the distance we can hear a whole lot of banging, bells and whistles, within minutes we see where all the noise is coming from – it is an Indian stag party! The kindly tuk-tuk driver who told us what was going on speaks excellent English, and has just earned himself a fare to the market. The fare that he quotes us is that low that we do not even bother negotiating, were talking pence not pounds.

Back at the market we wander around at our own pace, I buy some masala spice blends to take home, including one for chai that ends up sat in the cupboard at home for a few years... Somehow, we ended up in a miniature painting shop, no intention of buying but still ended up with a freebie that he drew whilst we were in there! The spending was not finished though, Alison found some cushion covers that she really liked - I could just envisage the decorating of the room to match this new colour scheme... With the sun dropping and darkness looming we take another tuk-tuk back to our home stay.

Showered and hungry we are in a quandary, last night the elderly owner had said he would make us a goat curry for this evening's meal, yet we had heard nothing more. Our plan was to go sit in the courtyard, have a beer and see what transpires. In our heart of hearts, we hope that he has forgotten, has gone out or is otherwise engaged – and just when we think we are off the hook he appears! Of course, being polite, we have no choice but to eat; the sauce is delicious to be fair but the goat is chewy and fatty. We manage to make a respectable dent into the portion he had brought out, and polish off the side dish – explaining that the rich gravy has left us full. With our table cleared he comes back out to sit with us, and before we know it, he is meditating. He is sat in the chair with his elbows resting on the arms, eyes closed and humming, his bristling moustache gently vibrating – we do not know where to look! Fortunately, we both manage to keep a straight face and the evening passes on quite normally....

After a good night's sleep and another leisurely breakfast, it is time to check-out and head to the airport, but not before big hugs and photographs with the very hospitable owners. It has been a great stay, once again accommodation that was in keeping with the surroundings and the history and heritage of the area. With our farewells made it was off to the airport, where my wind-up meerkat torch causes confusion at the baggage x-ray. Rather than my bag just appearing at the other side it is brought over and I am asked to empty it, the reason is a small plastic torch. With a quick demonstration ending with smiles all around we are through, waiting to board our flight to Mumbai.

By the time we reach Mumbai Alison was not feeling at her best, not sure what it was hopefully nothing worse than a twenty-four-hour bug of some kind, it came out of nowhere. She was awake enough though to see the huge slum areas by the side of the airport as we came into land, that is one vast site that must house thousands of residents in what seems like less than basic conditions. Our name was being held up on cardboard as we entered the arrivals lounge and in no time, we were being whisked away from the airport to our hotel, the glamorous sounding West End Hotel. As a result of being under the weather Alison ended up sleeping, or at least resting her eyes, most of the way from the airport to our hotel close to Marine Drive. I was fascinated, and amazed in equal measures as we drive over the huge bridge, or sea link as they call it that cuts across the bay. What a feat of engineering and such views! The traffic was not as manic as we expected, having said that it was a Saturday evening – so our journey across Mumbai went far smoother than we anticipated.

Whenever the car stopped at traffic lights vendors were offering to clean windscreens or wandering around to the side of the car, selling their wares; I did buy some travel magazines at one of our stops, I had noticed Kerala on the cover and we plan to visit there next year. Beggars, nearly all young children, were also swiftly moving between the cars, tapping on our windows and gesturing that they were hungry. It was sad to see and both awkward and uncomfortable at the same time, our driver said just to ignore them - but it was so difficult to look straight ahead and blank them. By the time we reached our hotel it was dark, Marine Drive looked fantastic all lit up, such a contrast and such a different side of Mumbai to what we had seen upon landing.

After enjoying two excellent heritage style hotels this one was very functional, an Indian version of Premier Inn. We were only here for the one night but as we headed back down to reception to look for somewhere to eat, we became aware that it was crowded with large groups of English men. It dawns on us then that England are playing cricket in the city, and with arriving in darkness we had not realised that the Wankhede stadium is just a five-minute's walk away. It was a surreal experience, in Udaipur and Jodhpur white faces were few and far between, any English spoken was with an Indian - in this hotel foyer it was like we had been transported via time travel all the way back home.

Alison was already feeling a little better, or at least of the opinion that something to eat would help. Feeling brave we wandered out, taking very careful note of where we had turned until we found the most unusual restaurant... There was a pizza restaurant, cooking and serving from the inside of an old bus. The tables were on the outside and what was formerly the front window of the coach had been modified to act as the serving hatch. Where the radiator had once been was being used to display all kinds of fruits, smoothies were their other main offering. The perfect meal, or at least the type of comfort food that we are looking for tonight – who would have thought that we would be sat in Mumbai experiencing the taste of Italy...

By the next morning we both had good appetites and the busy restaurant at the hotel was doing a roaring trade of full English breakfasts, and it was a decent attempt (apart from the horrible chicken sausages). Even once we had eaten there was still two hours before our tour guide was due to pick us up, so we went out exploring. We were shocked! There were so many people just laid out sleeping on the pavements, literally dozens; we were right next to a hospital so perhaps they were visiting people who were inpatients there, or even waiting to go in for an appointment themselves? It was a real revelation; Mumbai is such a contrast – some of the richest people on the planet living in touching distance of those who have next to nothing.

Once we reached the end of the road the Wankhede stadium was looming over everything else; it is vast – the biggest cricket stadium that we have ever seen. We go and investigate but can only get so close before being turned around by the local police as we do not have a match ticket. The Barmy Army are already making their way into the ground and we are quite envious; normally we only get excited about the cricket when it is the Ashes, but it would have been nice to have gone and watched the game. Unfortunately, that is not an option, for one we already have a tour planned and paid for, and two, we would need to leave for the airport before the days play is over. We make our way back to the hotel, the people sleeping on the paths are now beginning to stir and it does look like they have bathroom facilities available in the street, perhaps this a designated sleeping area? Before going on our tour today we need to check out of the hotel, so with our bags collected we get that done; our tour driver will be ferrying us to the airport as the final part of the days schedule. When we are collected from reception we are taken by surprise – we have never had a lady tour guide before, or at least not in India.

She is very organised, handing us an itinerary and telling us that a Sunday is a good day for a tour, getting around the city is so much easier! First stop is by the instantly recognisable railway station, the easy spelling and pronunciation is Mumbai Central, the official name is the Chhatrapati Shivaji Terminus. It was formerly known as the Victoria Terminus and as well as being a functioning (in fact the busiest in India) station, it is also a UNESCO World Heritage Site. It was designed by a British born architectural engineer, Frederick William Stevens - although the initial design was by Axel Haig, in a flamboyant Italian Gothic style. Construction began in 1878 and was completed in 1887, marking fifty years of Queen Victoria's rule. The name was changed from Victoria Terminus to Chhatrapati Shivaji in 1996. Mr Shivaji was a seventeenth century warrior king who fought the Mughal Empire. These days the terminus is the headquarters of India's Central Railway, and it is another one of those buildings that is so big it is impossible to get a complete photograph of.

Moving on from the station and onto the museum about Gandhi's life, Mani Bhavan. This modest two-storey house on the delightfully named Laburnum Road was Gandhi's Mumbai home come headquarters for nearly twenty years. The actual room where he slept during his stay is on the second floor, and although partitioned off with a Perspex screen you can witness the room exactly as it was, complete with his books and a basic bed laid out on the floor. It is an unusual museum, the story of his life, or at least the important stages are displayed in what I can only describe as like in the style of how we would represent a nativity scene. Little doll characters are displayed in cases with a few brief, but concise notes explaining what you are looking at, all very low-tech but a wonderful way of telling his story. Another room houses the library, containing over forty thousand reference books; these can be borrowed by scholars and teachers. Other books, stamps and personal effects are kept in glass cases for safe-keeping. Scattered all around the place are photographs of Gandhi, the images depict his life from his childhood through to his assassination. Press clippings and headlines from the newspapers of the time give an interesting take too; the way he is looked back upon and revered now wasn't always the case? I guess the saying that history will judge you is very apt, complex decisions and the subsequent outcomes often take a lot of years to bear fruition.

The story of the Indian flag is also explained with examples through the years. At the time of Imperial rule, it even had the Union Jack in the top left corner upon a dark red background. In 1921 it was Gandhi who first proposed the Indian National Congress flag. In the centre was a traditional spinning wheel, symbolising Gandhi's goal of making Indians self-reliant by producing their own clothing, the top third was white, the middle green and the bottom stripe red. Eventually the red was replaced with saffron and the stripes jiggled around to come up with what we now recognise as the colours of India. The saffron stood for courage and sacrifice, the white represented peace and truth, while the green meant faith and chivalry. It was only a month before India gained independence (fifteenth of August 1947), that the current flag became the standard, out went the spinning wheel to be replaced with the Ashoka Chakra (wheel) which represents the eternal wheel of law. What each colour represented also now changed... the Saffron now denotes renunciation or disinterestedness. The white in the centre is light, the path of truth to guide our conduct, whilst the green shows our relation to the soil and plant life, on which all other life depends. The 'wheel' in the centre was very busy, it still stood for the wheel of the law but now also denotes motion and the dynamism for a peaceful change.

Other highlights of the museum are that you can access the balcony from where Gandhi was removed upon his arrest back in 1932; the charge he faced was for encouraging a civil disobedience movement in the wake of emergency measures imposed by the British government. From the moment you enter Mani Bhavan and come face to face with the bust of Mahatma Gandhi you realise that you are in the presence of real history, this unassuming house is where the foundations were laid that created the India that we all recognise today. It is so much more than just a museum...

Our drive takes us around some tree lined fields by the universities, local cricket matches are being played out in front of spectators who are on their Sunday strolls. We head down to India Gate and the Taj Mahal hotel, today is exactly four years on from the terror attack that hit Mumbai and there is a peace rally going on at the Gate. We have a wander around, walking the length of the hotel, taking in the views. Access to any nearer India Gate is impossible, airport style security screening is required to enter and the queues are massive! Fortunately, both are plenty big enough to see from our distant vantage point anyway...

The Gateway of India was built to commemorate the arrival of King George V, Emperor of India. His visit on the second of December 1911 was the first visit of a British monarch to India. Unfortunately, George only got to see a cardboard model of the monument, construction did not begin until 1915! If its first part of history is slightly comical it has a second claim to fame. British Infantry passed through the Gateway with a twenty-one-gun salute, as part of a handover ceremony on the twenty-eighth of February 1948, signalling the end of the British Raj and its rule. The people of Mumbai are said to have mixed feelings about the Gate, some consider it as synonymous with the city, the first structure visible to visitors arriving by sea, while others see it as a symbol of conquest and colonisation.

A trip up to the Malabar Hills district and another Jain temple follows on our whistle stop tour of Mumbai's highlights. The temple is another white marble building, just like the one at Ranakpur, but the explosion of colour starts before you even get inside... Chalk boards outside list all the rules, what can and what cannot be taken into the temple. Ladies may not visit if they are menstruating. Leather items are all banned, you should not have eaten in the clothes that you are wearing, or have been the bathroom in! No chewing. There may be a lengthy list but at least they are all in colourful chalk writing... The inside of the temple (from what we can see) is very colourful, and the two elephant statues at the entrance are very impressive, but we had eaten breakfast in what we are wearing so couldn't enter, or at least not with a clear conscience!

As we enjoyed the views from Malabar Hill (this is where the wealthy citizens of the city live), our lady guide gave us more information on Jainism. Not only are its stricter followers completely vegan, they even extend that to not eating certain types of vegetables, it is a no to ginger, garlic, potato or onions for them, nothing with a root that has been pulled from the ground. It is all based on a principle of non-violence to living things, or ahimsa as they call it, and this even extends to pulling up living root vegetables - Jains believe in reincarnation and believe that all living things contain a soul, even the humble potato...

If we thought Jainism was a bit rule bound and odd, we were completely shocked when she told us about the Parsi community in Mumbai. They are a group of followers in India of the Persian prophet Zoroaster; Parsis, whose name means 'Persians,' are descended from the Persian Zoroastrians who emigrated to India to avoid religious persecution by the Muslims. Most of them now live in Mumbai and the villages around the outskirts. Parsis have a high literacy rate; in 2001 their literacy rate was nigh on ninety-eight percent, the highest of any Indian community, today the Persian connection is negligible, their mother tongue is Gujarati. According to the 2011 Census of India, there were around fifty-seven thousand Parsis in India, but demographic trends project that by 2020 the Parsis will number as few as twenty-three thousand.

When they arrived in India is highly speculative, but it is at least over one thousand years ago; they were welcomed and settled, but they really came to the fore with the arrival of the East India Company and the era of the British Raj. Many Parsis held prominent roles at this time, so after many years lost in obscurity and poverty, they finally met employers who valued their higher level of education and literacy. Now you may think what had us shocked by all of that? It is all to do with their funerals... When a Parsi passes away the priest comes to say prayers for the cleansing of sins and to affirm the faith of the deceased. Fire is brought into the room; prayers begin and the body is washed. The ceremony then begins, a circle is drawn around the body into which only the bearers may enter, they then carry the corpse to the cemetery, walking in pairs connected by white fabric. A dog is essential for the funeral process because it can see death. The body is taken to the top of the Tower of Silence at Doongerwadi (part of Malabar Hill where we are), for the vultures to feed upon, and once the bones have been stripped clean and bleached by the sun, they are pushed into the circular opening in the centre of the tower.

The reason behind this type of funeral is that Zoroastrian tradition considers human and animal corpses to be unclean, polluting. They consider earth, fire and water to be sacred elements so both burial or cremation are immediately ruled out, they would contaminate the ground or the flames respectively. Placing the bodies of the dead at the top of towers exposed to the sun and at the mercy of scavenging birds gives your body a final purpose, it feeds and nurtures, giving back, rather than being disposed of in a way that pollutes and contaminates. It may be a tradition that goes back thousands of years, but they have allowed for a modern twist - solar panels have been installed in the Towers of Silence to speed up the decomposition process! All a little grim as we looked over to where the guide was pointing, quite thankful that there was nothing we could see, luckily the trees were hiding the view of the tower...

On a lighter note, dhobi ghat was an amazing sight, for those of you who are not familiar it is Mumbai's famous laundry! Our first question is how does anything ever get back to its rightful owner? It looks crazy, impossible, surely no one can manage this much laundry and keep track of where it belongs? The name dhobi is the name given to the local washermen, and this place has been here for nearly one hundred and fifty years! This occupation has passed down from one generation to the next, around two hundred families are responsible for this laundry that handles roughly a half a million items a day! Its full name is the Mahalaxmi Dhobi Ghat, and we are here at prime time, early afternoon. Even on a Sunday the dhobis are in action, washing takes place in the morning and the early afternoons are the perfect time to see the clothes being dried.

Our guide explains how they are sorted by colour and put into soak, before being taken into one of the dozens of individual stone bays where they are washed by hand, the dhobis beating them on what they call the flogging stone. Thoroughly beaten, they then get a rinse before they are wrung out and folded, ready to be hung out to dry. Line upon line of washed clothes are then hung out to dry in a manner that optimizes both time and space, at this stage they are still in their respective colour groups. No space is spared, corrugated roofs, ground level – anywhere that a washing line can be installed. Finally, once dry they are taken in and ironed before being reassigned to their respective owners, all by means of a code that is written on the back or inner of each garment. We are told that it is an amazingly accurate and efficient service, one of the main reasons behind the ghat's popularity with the city's businesses.

Our official tour is over, and to be honest our first lady guide has excelled, it has been one of the best experiences we have had, friendly and informative throughout. With just over an hour or so before we need to head to the airport our driver, who also speaks excellent English seizes the moment to make a little extra for himself – did we fancy a tour of the slums? We were not going to turn down that opportunity, so we took him up on the offer and he escorted us into areas of the city that there is no way we would have dared to venture into alone.

He confirmed what our guide had already told us, we may look at them as slums and consider the living conditions as appalling but the people living there actually have everything they need. They have their own businesses, they have health services and are very self-efficient, in fact when the authorities offer them better housing on the outskirts of the city they never want to move. It is these tightly packed communities that they need to make money, the sheer quantity of people that enables them to make a good living. The alternative accommodation is not offered to improve or better their lives, it is more down to the value of the prime land that they occupy, as usual someone making big money is the real motive behind the scheme.

As we drive alongside a slum area, small square concrete rooms, two or three stories high go on for as far as the eye can see, the driver pulls over and points out the small extensions overhanging the river. Describing them, I would say they look like man-sized bird boxes, one small opening and a sloping roof hanging precariously from the wall. If I said that they were about the size of a toilet cubicle you would know exactly what they were, no fancy plumbing here – from bottom, literally, to the river in a matter of seconds. The smell was a little ripe...

Once parked up we walk to see a small spice grinding operation, it was so noisy and hard to breathe such was the pleasant but pungent smell of the powders being produced. Further into the depths we head and pottery was being produced, simple clay vessels lined up everywhere, some looked like cooking pots, complete with lids whilst others looked like bowls and vases. We were shown into someone's home, and apart from it being hugely overcrowded (that one room was the whole house) it was clean, shoes all lined up by the door, beds made etc. This 'bonus' trip that the driver offers is obviously something that he does on a regular basis, but regardless of that it has given us an insight into how they live and has taken us into areas of the city that we have only ever seen on TV before. Thankfully, our driver knew his way back out of the maze of alleyways, there is not a chance in the world that we could have ever found our way back to the car! Unfortunately for us that is our time in Mumbai up, or at least for now - it would be somewhere that we would happily visit again, and still have plenty more to see and take in. The airport beckons, and finally we will get to Goa and unwind...

What we did, and where we ate in Goa remains a bit of a mystery for this visit, unfortunately we have somehow lost, or misplaced the DVD or memory stick that all the pictures had been downloaded to. Luckily, we were still 'old school' at this time, so we do have the best ones that had been developed and put in an album, so the Rajasthan and Mumbai photos exist but unfortunately no others. It goes without saying that we enjoyed it just as much as previously, as on our return home we booked a repeat visit for the following November. If you remember we had already been delayed for over twenty-four hours on the way out? Our delays were not over yet, the return flight was also late leaving, only by about four hours this time though! As much as this was a complete nightmare at the time, the compensation award more than made up for it – our claims for delays to both legs of the flight were successful, we received recompense of more than what we had paid for the entire holiday.

April 2013 - Kerala and Kanyakumari

April, and it is a holiday of many firsts; this was to be our first ever escorted tour, a multi-centre holiday taking in some of the highlights that Kerala has to offer. It was also the first time that we had ever flown with a scheduled airline rather than on the usual Thomson, Thomas Cook or Monarch chartered flight. The lists of firsts continued, it was the first time that we had a lady tuk-tuk driver, and it was definitely the first time that we had ever been served beer with the bottle wrapped up in old newspaper!

We were really looking forward to this holiday, not only for the chance to explore a different resort but we were also expecting a different vibe, or feel to the place. Goa very much has a stranglehold for beach holidays aimed at western tourists, much of that is down to its Portuguese influence and history. In Kerala we get the chance to see how an Indian state differs, for better or worse. We had heard stories of beer being not so readily available, or clandestinely being served in teapots, an undercover drinking operation that intrigued us. We had also seen rave reviews about the sea food, the usual diet of two curries a day will change for this holiday?

This would also be a more back to nature trip, no forts or palaces and all that marble, granite and sandstone. No ancient kingdoms like at Hampi, with lists of dates and unpronounceable names to try and remember. Natural beauty will be the order of the day this time, lakes and rivers, national parks and wildlife, the tea plantations and the mountains of the Western Ghats. Chinese fishing nets and ancient Kathakali dancing – the list goes on, and that is all to come before we reach the beach stay part of the experience. Knowing our low tolerance for resting and relaxing we plan to arrange ourselves a trip to Kanyakumari, the southernmost point of India in Tamil Nadu.

Mercury Holidays, or Mercury Direct as it was back then, was who we had booked it through, our flight was with Emirates, and better than we had imagined – we were expecting good things but it was amazing. If you remember, we had travelled with Monarch just a few years back, this was a different world! Thomas Cook and Thomson flights were ok, but they had already got to the stage of charging for headphones for a limited entertainment package. Here everything was on tap and free, you could create your own playlist from hundreds of albums, TV wise (and it was a good-sized TV), there were films, documentaries, comedy box sets, sporting channels, games options – you name it they had it covered. The food was excellent, with a choice of mains from the menu and the complimentary drinks were being served on a regular basis. We were feeling a little pampered.

Upon our arrival at Trivandrum airport, we were taken to Kovalum where we would spend our first night at the Uday Samudra Hotel, tomorrow we would be picked up and our tour would begin properly. The Uday Samudra was a lovely hotel, far more luxurious than the kind of place that we would usually stay at, but for us there was to be no unpacking. Even when we finished our tour, we would only come back here to pick up our cases. The Hotel Samudra, also in Kovalum, was where the beach part of our stay would be spent. Not wanting to get our costumes wet we went off and explored the beaches that were to hand. Kovalum is a lovely place, two or three little beaches in secluded bays and an attractive lighthouse at the far end, painted with red and white hoops.

Whilst there are no beach shacks there are a handful of restaurants on the promenade serving both food and drinks, so any concerns about this being a dry holiday are immediately put to rest. Our first impressions are good, we like it here. It is quite different to Goa but not in a bad way – and anyway why would we visit somewhere new hoping that it is the same as a previous holiday? Variety makes the world go round. Our biggest concern is that some of the restaurants in Kovalum look to have closed for the season, so our eating options are looking more limited than what we are used to.

As it happens, we don't leave the hotel for food that first night, a massive thunderstorm and torrential rain put paid to any plans. This was to become a theme of our evenings in Kerala, or at least the nights when we were on the coast. Fortunately, we learned that the rain subsided as quickly as it had blown in, so other nights we held off and went out an hour later, albeit exceedingly hungry! Breakfast had the full Indian breakfast options alongside omelettes, cereals and English style fry up, so we were spoiled for choice. The hoppers were particularly tasty, we had eaten them once before in Sri Lanka, and have since found out that Southern Indian and Sri Lankan dishes have a lot in common, many featuring on the menus of both countries.

Suitably full and our driver picks us up for the long journey to Alleppey, the road looks familiar as we head out back past the airport from where we had been collected from yesterday. It is about four hours before we arrive and our shown to our traditional rice boat. The crew are very welcoming and in no time the ropes are being untied ready to set sail, we were half expecting to be sharing the boat with other guests but there is just us and a crew of three. We never see much of Alleppey, which is a shame – on the coastal side is the Arabian Sea and the lakes and lagoons join it from the other – apparently it is a quaint little town in its own right, but more famous as being the starting point of the backwaters, a bit like Wroxham for the Norfolk Broads back home, but with more sun.

The house boat that we, and hundreds of others are travelling on are known locally as 'kettuvallam'. In their day they were traditional rice barges, so due to that they are each similar in length, about twenty-four metres. A simple reconfiguration and there are room for a pair of bedrooms, bathroom facilities, cooking quarters and a comfortable seating area where you can look out for wildlife and wave to the locals as you explore the canals. The boats themselves are made from jackwood and coated with a black resin made by boiling cashew nut shells. The jackwood is a rain forest species of the laurel family, found mainly in eastern Australia these days, the canopy and living quarters are all made from coir rope, cleverly building in doorways, window frames and even air-conditioning vents into the knitted like design.

The wetlands have all been reclaimed from what was once one big lake, Vembanadu; as usual in India it did not happen overnight, the project started in 1832 and by the end of 1984 approximately two-thousand three-hundred hectares of land has been reclaimed. The concept behind the idea was to convert these wetlands into fertile paddy fields, providing much needed rice for the local people. Two thirds of the area that has been reclaimed are now rice paddy fields, but in creating that many big and small canals have been formed, so accidentally they created a bi-product - a boat tourist industry that draws plenty of visitors to the state. Either side of these crisscrossed canals and rivers are beautiful lagoons, coconut palms, lush green paddy fields and local village homes and temples. The local communities live on the banks of the canals, these waterways are their roads and pavements, each house probably has a boat of some kind to get themselves around, the children to school and to fetch their weekly shop. A water taxi / bus service also runs up and down, so in some ways it is not that dissimilar to life on land. It is obvious that tourists also play a big part in the local people's lives, perhaps a little shop on land at a point where they know the boats moor up for the night? Even a moving shop, a small boat selling locally produced items and souvenirs to the passing visitors?

We are loving the tranquillity of the place, once away from Alleppey itself the rice boats all spread out and meander their way around various routes to such an extent that you feel alone in your own little bubble. The food is delicious and just keeps on coming, maybe no one has told the chef that only one room is occupied, there is only us two on board, not four people! As for exercise, lots of waving at passers by going about their daily routines, and using the water in so many ways. The local children look to be having the most fun, splashing around at the sides, swimming and playing... but equally it could just be bath time? We see people washing a multitude of things as we sail by, their own hair, pots and pans, clothing, preparing vegetables are all on our film clips. With the sky turning orange and the sun setting we head away from the tight canals and out onto the lake for our mooring for the night. Another huge feed is spread out before us, and we do our best to eat our way through it; the small fish with lots of little bones are nibbled at politely before being pushed to one side... Daytime had been fascinating, watching the world go by, every few minutes something would catch our eye and grab our attention – but now it is completely black bar the odd twinkling lights from other house boats at their moorings and the stars in the sky.

It should have been an early night for us, there's no Madhu's here to keep us up until last orders; the staff aboard were already asleep, laying down in the corridor beyond our cabin was their hard bed for the night. We used the bathroom and got ourselves tucked in under the smallest duvet we have ever had, I am certain that we have seen bigger bath towels! It did not take us long to realise that we were in for a chilly night, the air conditioning was on and we had no remote to change the setting; looking out of our cabin the crew are fast asleep so of no assistance. Reluctant to wake them, we go into our overnight bag and put on the two sets of clothes that we have with us!

By morning the sun was back out and the temperature rising, apart from very crumpled clothing we were both feeling good, and despite last night's food mountain, we were ready for breakfast. Washed and teeth cleaned we go sit at the table, waiting for our food - and when asked how we slept, were we comfortable, we both just nod politely and say everything was fine, not wanting to say that we had been frozen initially but were reluctant to disturb them...

We were back on the move even before the breakfast plates had been cleared, so we were both looking out, eyes peeled for wildlife. Other than the usual cormorants and egrets we did not see much of excitement, we were hoping for a glimpse of a kingfisher (the bird, not the beer), but were out of luck. Chickens and goats were parading around on the banks, the goats chewing at thick gorse and tarpaulins if nothing else was available. The local children were making their way to school, waiting for the boat at certain places before boarding with the rest of their classmates, all looking smart in their uniforms even though they are washed in the murky canal. Like a scene from Wacky Races all the rice boats converge as they make their way back to Alleppey, it is as if all canals lead there as we go from travelling solo to joining a huge convoy that are returning, no doubt to be reloaded with more tourists and another wheelbarrow load of food. It was a relaxing experience, but the one night had been enough to give us a taste of life on the backwaters, for us it was onto Cochin once we had disembarked.

It was a short drive to Cochin, an hour and a half at most before we were safely delivered to our next accommodation, the Sreeragam Luxury Villa Retreat – the word luxury summed it up perfectly. Our room was more of a suite, the table and living quarters and bedroom divided by a beautiful modern stained-glass door. The bathroom was great, the option of a jacuzzi bath or a shower that had jets at all heights and lit up like a 1980s disco. Outside was a circular plunge pool with an elephant's head and trunk providing a very Indian themed water feature. The only downside was that we were the only guests.

On our arrival we had been adorned with garlands and offered a welcome drink, and while our passports were being photocopied the lady was telling us about the local village and that once we had freshened up, she would arrange a trip for us to explore the local area. We do as she suggests, so with our cases dropped off in our room we head back down to the foyer. To our surprise she picks up the keys herself and leads us outside to the green tuk-tuk parked in the corner, were we being sexist in thinking that she would ring for a man to take us out? The short tour was genuine fun, bombing up and down little country roads with no other traffic in sight. First stop was the local school, the very same school that she had attended so she knew these parts like the back of her hands. A wooden temple was the next stop, a strange type of building, but we were to see more just like it on this tour of Kerala, perhaps it's a local design. Rather than the wooden frame being on the inside of the temple it is on the outside, effectively creating numerous shelves from ground level right up to the roof in a grid effect.

Having left the hub of the village we head further out into the countryside and see one of the biggest banyan trees yet, there is something about them that intrigues us. They are different to other trees in so many ways, not least that they grow roots downwards from a great height, these are known as arial prop roots, and over time they become indistinguishable from the primary trunk. What we never knew is that in Hinduism, the leaf of the banyan tree is said to be the resting place for the god Krishna, and are also part of folklore in both Vietnam and the Philippines. As we make our way back to the villa, we pull to the side of the road to watch some bathing buffaloes, huge great creatures that are cooling themselves off by wallowing in the mud – and you cannot have a buffalo without the obligatory egret perched upon its back, feeding on the bugs and insects!

Our evening is to be spent at the Kerala Kathakali Centre, try saying that after a drink or two... In all honesty it is not really our cup of tea, storytelling in the form of traditional dance, from experience that sounds like a lot of drumming and arms wafting with us not understanding what is happening. Regardless, it is included in our tour, already paid for and you never know, this could be the one form of local dance that we enjoy - I am not holding my breath though...

Cochin is just a short drive away and the Kerala Kathakali Centre is right in the heart of the city, a stone's throw from the beach. The theatre had been renovated in 2010, with an innovative design and layout, using traditional temple and church architecture from ancient times. It is a classic wooden building that prides itself on having excellent acoustics, and promises us 'talented performers that make for an unforgettable experience.' What is helpful, and gives us half a chance of following what is happening is a paper brochure that tells us what fables we are going to see, complete with a brief outline of the story. So tonight, if our interpretation of hand gestures and eye movements are a little off, we will still have a picture of the tale that they are trying to convey. The list of sketches looks a bit long for my liking.

We have some of the best seats in the house, front row and central. When we first arrive, they are doing their make-up - right there on the stage in front of us. When I say make-up think extreme face painting, except with more green colouring involved than in an Incredible Hulk tribute. Once they had done what they could of their own faces they took turns at finishing off each other's, the result was impressive. As they left the stage to put on costumes something bizarre was happening to us, we were looking forward to the show. After a few minutes a bare-chested drummer pushed his way through the curtains and took his place, the show was on.

Exactly what each scene represented has long gone from our memory, but with the aid of the literature we had managed to follow (and enjoy) what we were seeing. The drummer and a 'singer' produced all the noise and sound effects to accompany the actions, the actors themselves are completely silent, telling the story solely through expressions. The eye movements were amazing, and for once we genuinely felt like we were 'reading' the script and performance as they were intending. Each sketch was a matter of a few minutes long, so what had initially looked an intimidating index of scenes to sit through flew by; for us the length was exactly right, enough without overdoing it. I am sure we have all been there at some point, where you start looking at your watch wishing it were all over!

The history of Kathakali goes back to around the seventeenth century, but its roots reach further back to the temple and folk arts of south-west India, so in some form it is traceable back for time immemorial. Kathakali is a 'story play' genre of art distinguished by the elaborately colourful make-up, costumes and face masks that the traditionally male actor-dancers wear, and is one of the eight classical dances of India. A combination of music, vocals and choreography in the form of hand and facial gestures are used to express ideas and emotions. Kathakali also incorporates movements from ancient Indian martial arts and athletic traditions to recount folk stories, religious legends and spiritual ideas from the Hindu classics.

Kathakali has the most elaborate of costumes, consisting of head dresses, face masks and vividly painted faces. It is the colourful outfits that have made Kathakali's popularity extend beyond adults, with children absorbed by the colours, make-up, light and sound of the performance. The colour of the make-up follows a traditional code, so connoisseurs amongst the audience can easily distinguish between the characters. The face paints are made up from vegetables and rice pastes, so all very natural. Because of the minimalistic way the show is performed it is said to be one of the most difficult styles to execute on stage, training young artists takes several years before they get a chance to go on stage. The actors 'speak' using a sign language; mudras are the hand movements and navarasas the facial expressions. If that sounds simple enough there are twenty-four 'mudras' and nine 'navarasas' (no idea what the plural of that is). The beat of the drum and the vocalist then have to work in harmony with the signs being expressed on stage to depict the story line being told.

After a great night's sleep, it is back into Cochin for our city tour. It is a city of two halves, on one hand there is the historic side dating all the way back to the fourteenth century when it was an important spice trading port on the west coast of India, central to business with Arab merchants from the pre-Islamic era. By 1505 the Portuguese had also established trading ports in Cochin, and many of the two-storey buildings from this period remain by the riverside. Across the river and it is a different world, very modern, all high rise living and office blocks. Although it is not the state capital of Kerala it is the most important hub for financial, commercial and industrial enterprises in the south of India. As well as a busy commercial port it is also home to the Southern Naval Command of the Indian Navy and the Indian Coast Guard with an attached air squadron.

We will be sticking to the old part of the city, the Queen of the Arabian Sea as it was once known, exploring various places of importance, admiring the murals painted following the tsunami of 2004 and having a go at catching fish on the old Chinese fishing nets. The streets are tight and busy but in a comfortable way, our guide takes us up to the rooftop of a shop so we can get a view from high up. The buildings are all very uniform in both height and width, neat tiled roofs and arranged in a grid pattern. He explains how these all date back to the fifteenth century and were built by the Portuguese spice merchants. Sitting just beyond the two rows of these barns is the river and an ugly great cruise liner the only blemish to a view that has remained constant for over five hundred years. When I say the only thing, it is safe to assume that the usual tangle of wires on telegraph poles were not their either, but at least they subtly blend in...

Within a short walking distance, we arrive at the Paradesi Synagogue, which is more generally known as the Cochin Jewish Synagogue. Our guide informs us that although we are still in the Old Quarter, we are now in what is known as Jew Town. The synagogue was built in 1568 for the flourishing Jewish community that had arrived from Portugal. These Sephardi Jews (the name given to Judaism followers from the Iberian Peninsula) were fleeing religious persecution in Spain and Portugal and settled here as the spice trade took off. The word Paradesi is used in several Indian languages, meaning 'foreigners.' This is the only one of the original seven synagogues in the area that is still in use.

The Jewish community has a big part in Cochins long history, the Malabari Jews (also known as Cochin Jews) created a prosperous trading community in Kerala, to such an extent that they were responsible for a major portion of the worldwide spice trade. The first synagogue in India was built in the fourth century when the Jews were already active merchants in south India along the Malabar coast. The Sephardi and the Malabari Jews shared many aspects of their religion, but the newcomers from Portugal retained their own culture and language for at least three more centuries. By 1660 Cochin was under Dutch rule, and known as Dutch Malabar – and the melting pot of Jews was added to further by them. These days the Paradesi Synagogue has three classes of members - White Jews are descendants of the original Sephardim from Spain, Portugal and a few additions from the Netherlands. The Black Jews (or Malabari Jews), are the original Jewish settlers of Cochin. The third group are the Meshuchrarim, their descendants of freed slaves brought over to India by the Sephardim. And there was us thinking this was a 'back to nature' trip with no dates and facts and figures involved...

Having had a lesson in Indian Jewish heritage we moved on to the Santa Cruz Cathedral Basilica. In some ways it is quite fortunate that it has survived to this day, the Dutch destroyed most Catholic buildings in the time of their rule. The foundation stone of the Santa Cruz church was laid in 1505, and legend has it that it was on the feast day of the Invention of the Holy Cross, hence the name. It was elevated to a Cathedral by Pope Paul IV in 1558 before receiving a further upgrade when in 1984 Santa Cruz was proclaimed a Basilica by Pope John Paul II. These days it is considered as one of the most important heritage sites of Kerala, and one of the finest and most impressive churches in India, visited by tourists the entire year-round. It remains as a place of devotion alongside its role of historic significance, endowed with architectural and artistic grandeur of the gothic style, perhaps the finest example to be found in the whole of India. All would have been lost if the Dutch had not needed it for their arms store...

Another church and the only other survivor of the Dutch purge on Catholic buildings is our next port of call. Where the Santa Cruz Cathedral looked resplendent in white, the Church of Saint Francis looked tired and weather beaten. We are not here to admire the grandeur of this building (which would have been difficult), but more for its historical importance. Built in 1503 it is one of the oldest European buildings in the whole of India, and for fourteen years was the burial place of the great explorer Vasco da Gama. Vasco da Gama was a Portuguese explorer, and the first European to reach India by sea in 1498. In many ways Da Gama's discovery of the sea route to India opened the gates to colonial empires, first by the Portuguese but eventually other European powers who wanted some of the same. Access to the Indian spice routes boosted the economy of the Portuguese Empire, at the heart of it were pepper and cinnamon, previously unknown to Europeans. Within a century the Dutch Republic and England had a finger in the pie, and a few years later France had joined the three other big players at the table.

In 1524 da Gama was appointed as Governor of India, and given the title of Viceroy. It was that same year he met his demise; setting sail in April, with a fleet of fourteen ships, it would be his third and final journey to India. After a troubled voyage in which four or five of the starting fleet had been lost, he arrived in India in September. Upon arrival Vasco da Gama immediately used his newly appointed powers to impose a new order in Portuguese India, replacing all the old officials with his own appointments. Whilst travelling around doing all this hiring and firing Gama unfortunately contracted malaria and subsequently died in Cochin, on Christmas Eve 1524. Vasco da Gama's body was promptly buried at the Church of Saint Francis before his remains were excavated and returned to Portugal in 1539.

That is it, buildings, dates and history lessons over, we make our way back down to the river to visit the Chinese fishing nets and the fish market by the side of them. This way of fishing is very unusual in India and almost unique to the area, it was first introduced by Chinese explorers who landed here in the fourteenth century. One interpretation of why the city is called Cochin is even linked to these nets; 'co-chin', means 'like China.' The best way to describe these nets is as giant hammocks on a pulley system with a ten-metre-high pivot. One end of the rope is attached to large rocks, acting as anchors in taking the weight and keeping the net horizontal once it has been lowered to the correct depth. The net can be raised by pulling on the ropes, usually done by a team of six fishermen – the nets are lowered and raised every few minutes to bring up the catch. These days there are as many tourists as fishermen, and most of their income comes through tips – after all visitors want to give it a go for themselves! As well as being a great photo opportunity it was good fun to have a try, there is no doubt that it would be a tiring job, there is a lot of weight to the wooden beams that the nets are attached to. As for our catch, nothing to write home about...

The stalls selling fish had some real whoppers, we can only assume that they have been caught further out at sea by more modern methods. It is one thing that we do enjoy wherever we are in the world, a good look at the local fish market. The selection is varied, on the floor are a couple of washing up bowls with tiny fish – like the ones we lifted out. The table at the front has prawns of varying sizes, from large to very large – bigger than anything we have ever tried in Goa. Behind them is the bigger stuff, three-foot long probably, no idea what they would be. The array of colours? Nothing overly exotic or vibrant, no finding nemo, but more delicate shades of pink, blue and yellow.

As we walk beyond the fish market, we notice the murals on the wall – depicting the tsunami of Boxing Day 2004. We had honeymooned in Sri Lanka in 2006 and the devastation was still there to be seen, thousands of people were still living under tarpaulins in makeshift homes having lost everything. Kerala (and southern India) had got lucky, there were casualties but nothing like the numbers of people that had been lost in Indonesia, Sri Lanka or Thailand. The pictures had all been done by the local children, so while there had been no casualties in Cochin itself it must have been a scary situation as the roads were turned into rivers.

Back at the Villa we took the opportunity to cool off in the plunge pool, Alison somehow misjudging her entry and soaking the book that she was about to read. It is strange what you remember, the funny moments always stand out... We really enjoyed our stay here, and here is our thoughts at the time...

Stunning hotel

Review of Sreeragam Luxury Villa Retreat

When we were being driven there, we began to worry! It is down some windy lanes & you wonder where you are being taken. Once you arrive you are made so welcome, the rooms are stunning, very different & very luxurious - never seen such big fluffy bath towels. There are some huge sunbeds in the (small but perfectly manicured) grounds plus a plunge pool / spa. The food was fantastic, breakfast amazing & nothing was too much trouble. Only negative is that if you want to explore from here, you need a taxi to get to Cochin - a good 10-minute ride away. If you just want to relax can't think of anywhere better.

We leave the city confines of Cochin and head out into the countryside and the rolling Cardamom hills, our destination is Thekkady and the Periyar National Park. On route we decide that the reason they have so many gods and deities in India is to protect them from crazy drivers. Anyone who has visited Goa will know that the rules of the road are just there to be ignored, it seems the same applies even when you are climbing up into the hills amongst tea plantations. The roads are narrow, with big drops on one side, hairpin bend after hairpin bend as you spiral your way up – but in India that does not mean no overtaking or adapting your driving. We are going slow to steady, it is a steep incline for us – those coming down are flying around corners, as usual in India any side of the road will do. As we hang on, almost considering which God to adopt our driver just laughs...

After what seems like forever (about four hours), we finally get a break from gripping our seats and a much-needed opportunity to stretch our legs. For the last thirty minutes or so we have been in tea plantation country, watching the local pickers with their baskets taking off the top three leaves from the plants, a welcome distraction from looking at the road and potential death! As well as being one of the bigger plantations with an outlet shop there are also restaurant and bathroom facilities at the Carady Goody Estate.

Our guide tells us a little about the place, of how the land owners built a fully functioning village for their workforce. As well as providing them with housing and schools they included a place of worship with a (attractive) catholic church for their day off. The views from here are vast, cars on the roads below shining in the sunlight and then just tea and more tea plants. There is something about tea plantations that are very pleasing on the eye, the manicured bushes and pathways always remind me of the marking on a giraffe, the bushes form quite irregular patterns but are always similar in size. Moving around between the plants are ladies with their headscarves on, protecting them from the overhead sun, their wicker baskets strapped to their backs – we had a go at tea picking in Sri Lanka once, and it is a lot harder than what it looks.

When in Rome and all that; a cup of tea at the extremely popular restaurant that is doing a roaring trade before visiting the bathroom. The on-site shop is selling freshly picked tea, at a good discount too apparently. Other locally produced products are also lining the shelves – coffee powder, pepper, cardamom and any other spices that are processed in the AVT groups factory. There is also a range of home-made chocolates, but we have always found the versions they have in India to be very grainy, even when its Cadburys, a totally different recipe to what we enjoy on a far to regular basis at home!

Seatbelts on and fingers crossed we are back on the road, only another half hour until we reach our destination, the Aranya Nivas KTDC hotel in Thekkady. The KTDC stands for Kerala Tourism Development Corporation, these are state government owned hotels and they regulate the standards of service and activities offered to visitors. Interestingly, they came about after Kerala Tours (in the early 1960's) went into partnership with Thomas Cook, popularising the hippie culture on Kovalum Beach to western countries. The Keralan government tried to nationalize Kerala Tours but could not because of legal issues, so instead it started its own version - known as Kerala Tourism Development Corporation (KTDC) in 1966.

Aranya Nivas describes itself as an 'authentic jungle lodge,' an exaggerated claim for a property in the Periyar National Park! Periyar itself is a protected tiger reserve, although it does openly admit that you would be extremely fortunate to see one. The park is set amongst the delightfully named Cardamom Hills of the south western Ghats, close to the border with Tamil Nadu. It was initially designated as a National Park, not for a tourist attraction but to prevent further encroachment by tea plantations, putting an end to their destruction of rare and endangered floras and faunas. Lake Periyar was created by damming the Periyar and Pamba rivers, providing a constant source of water for the local wildlife that inhabit this green area.

Whilst tigers are an unlikely sighting, we should expect to see elephants, wild boars, the Indian giant squirrel and various other primates. Although they are active in the park, we are hoping NOT to see either the king cobra or the Malabar pit viper – three- to four-metre-long venomous snakes are just not our thing. As we head to our rooms there are signs everywhere, warning guests to keep doors and windows closed, the local monkeys are notorious for getting inside rooms at any opportunity. Maybe calling itself a jungle lodge is not so far off the mark.

Its already getting dark but we still have time for a quick wander around the grounds of the Aranya Nivas, and within minutes have our first sighting of the giant squirrels. Although they are slightly larger than the grey version we get at home, it's hardly significant – when it was called 'giant' I was hoping for one at least the size of a large house cat. Long-tailed squirrel would have been a better description. The monkeys were also about in force, high up in the trees; two distinct types, one lot was very black and the other more the 'standard' monkey – my primate describing is not the greatest. As we are heading back in near darkness, we have an unexpected meeting with a wild boar, wisely we decide to give it a wide berth as its rooting around a seating bench.

Next morning it is all very misty, which is disappointing as in a few hours' time we have a boat trip on the lake, hoping to spot some of the local bird life and elephants by the shore – fingers crossed it will have lifted a little by the time we board. We retrace our steps from yesterday, enjoying an early morning walk when we bump into a large group of Indian children, as usual they are keen to speak to us, an opportunity to practise their already good English. They love to have their photographs taken, both with their friends and with us; they are keen to look at them on the screen of the camera, perhaps they don't get to see many photographs of themselves? We spend a good ten minutes chatting with them before they are rounded up by a group of Nuns and they head off in the other direction. They were really nice children, so polite and inquisitive and a real pleasure to meet and converse with.

Luckily, the mist is lifting, and by the time we climb aboard the boat called Jalaraja the lake is looking mysterious and eerie. The sun is trying to break through so all looks set for a nice sailing, but even before we set off, we realise how low the lake is. We set sail and before long we spot a hornbill on one of the hundreds of protruding trees, our guide says it is a Malabar grey hornbill, and the protruding perch it is sat on is part of the forest that was submerged when the dam was built. The lake is smooth, not a ripple on it and with the sun by now breaking through perfect mirror images are formed, hopefully we can get some good photos. We gently chug our way around the lake, elephants are grazing to one side and then as we turn the corner, we see a group of wild boars at the water's edge. In no time the boars and elephants are both replaced with some big groups of sambars, a large deer native to this part of India. We decide that the lake being so low on water is actually a good time to visit, it looks like when it is full it reaches right up to the edge of the forest, so the animals would be so much more difficult to spot.

Whilst we do not get to see a tiger, we do spot a herd of gaurs, also known as the Indian bison. The gaur is the largest breed of wild cattle, but unfortunately classed as a vulnerable species with numbers declining rapidly. Part of their problem is brought about by an ever-declining habitat, they are largely confined to evergreen forests with hilly terrain that has good availability of water. It is estimated that there is up to a thousand of them living in Periyar, and with the elusive tiger their only predator in this park hopefully they can continue to thrive. As we head back towards the jetty, we see plenty more bird life, but nothing overly colourful or exciting – the usual cormorants and egrets.

That is another part of our tour over with, and our review at the time explains why we cannot remember anything about our meals there – describing as alright is our polite way of saying disappointing!

Amazing location makes up for tired rooms

Review of Aranya Nivas KTDC

Location is fantastic, set-in grounds with the monkeys, giant squirrels & other wildlife. Perfect place to get the early morning lake cruise from, just 30 seconds walk from the front door. the rooms were alright, well equipped (flat screen TV's etc) but just in need of some TLC. Maybe it was the end of the season but they were a bit tired - but clean. Food at the hotel was alright, main restaurant buffet style but there was a room service menu.

The final stop of our tour was the leg that we had both been looking forward to most, but also equally apprehensive about at the same time. A home stay; is that a place in the spare bedroom, or something grander, like a Granny flat – we are not sure what to expect. Having survived the journey once more back down the winding roads without a head on collision or even a near miss we are in a relaxed mood, accommodation has all been excellent so far, so we are cautiously optimistic. As we pull up outside that confidence has been well placed, it is a beautiful building – very ornate and traditional.

Our hosts are very welcoming, the whole family greet us upon our arrival and our case is taken by the eldest son, putting it in our room ready for us. They explain how we will eat in the house with them and be shown around the local area. As an added bonus the Pooram Gajamela, or the 'Festival of Elephants' is on tonight in nearby Elanthoor – our hosts want to take us to that, and have even arranged access to a balcony on the main street to view the parade from. Our room itself is in a wing attached to the main house and it looks like there is a second guest room next door to us, the rooms are simply furnished but stunning.

It is the furnishings that add a warm touch of colour to the room, all wooden from the beds to the chairs and made from locally grown teak and mahogany, after all, it is an eco-stay. The rooms are whitewashed and with a high ceiling, making them feel nice and cool as well as incredibly spacious. A mini bar is tucked away and there is also air-conditioning, should we need it. They explain that the traditional design of the wooden ceiling contains ancient ventilation techniques that are superior to modern units. Time will tell...

The younger son asks if we want a tour of the local village, we are more than happy to take him up on that offer... by the time we have got to the end of the street we are being led by both him and five of his mates! They all speak particularly good English and are full of questions, we are getting a proper interrogation here, how long are we here for? What other countries have we visited? Do we have children? We get a slight reprieve as we come to the water pump and the questions are replaced with a demonstration of how it works; next stop is the rubber plantation and a fantastic explanation of the procedure, especially considering his age (perhaps nine or ten years old) and it is in his second language.

Rubber tapping is a non-harmful way of collecting latex from a rubber tree. The tree needs to be around six years in age and have a six-inch diameter to be suitable, the latex is released by slicing a small groove into the bark of the tree and peeling back the bark. He explains how the 'tapping' is done after sunset or in the early morning, avoiding the heat of the day. We assumed that was to make life easier for the workers, but it is because the latex will drip longer at lower temperatures, up to five hours, before coagulating and sealing the cut. The next night (or morning), the other side of the tree can be cut to harvest from that side. The latex dribbles down the small groove and is collected in a bowl tied around the trunk, the bowl that we are looking at looks suspiciously like a coconut shell... upcycling at its absolute best! Because there is no need to cut down the tree the bark will regrow and the process can be repeated time and again – all very clever.

After a brief return to the home stay, we are taken back out in the family car, there is a vibrant pink church for us to look at and a trip down to the river. As usual in India the river is the hive of local activity and a communal meeting place – be that as a leisure facility, bathroom or kitchen. It is also where the village dragon boat is housed; we have struck gold with the timing of the Festival of Elephants, so to be here at the exact time of the dragon boat racing would be lucky beyond belief. We do get to look at the boat under its canopy and are astonished by its length, but then we are told that when it comes to the racing festival you can fit up to one hundred and fifty rowers in a single boat! We do opt for a slower boat ride; we take the local ferry across the river and back.

Our evening meal is served at the big table in the main house and we are the only guests as it is just the family and us. The spread we are served is huge, but more in a tapas style than popping to your local Indian restaurant - I think the idea is to try as many local dishes as possible rather than select one dish. We will not be leaving here hungry as the food keeps on coming, if a bowl is emptied then another one swiftly replaces it. I manage to make a fool of myself as they are asking what we are doing next, once we are back in Kovalum. I was telling them that we are planning to book a tour to visit Kanyakumari, the southernmost tip of India ... except I get confused and call it Kalamaki, (the tourist hotspot on the Greek island of Zante), no wonder they were looking blankly at me! What an idiot!

We head back to our room to get changed ready for this evening's festival, and then join them back at the main house. Its back in the car for the short journey to Elanthoor where we are taken completely by surprise, this festival is massive – we were expecting a village fete style event. Elanthoor is lit up like Blackpool illuminations, there are windmills with moving sails, trees all decorated and images of various Gods all made up in lights. Once we are parked up, we are led up some steps and onto a balcony overlooking the high street. What a vantage point! We can already see lights in the distance so the procession won't be that long before it reaches here. As it gets closer, we realise that the lights were in fact flames, the drums getting louder and louder before we can make out the elephants through the darkness. They look magnificent, decked out with jewelled cloths covering their foreheads and trunks, the mahout riding high on its neck under a coloured umbrella with silver tinsel hanging from it.

By this stage the procession is upon us, the flames are being carried by hundreds of men at the front. The flames burn brightly, some in the shape of an upturned horse shoe, others just from a plain lit stick. The mahouts are all bare chested and some of the elephants have additional headgear, like a crown in the shape of a shield, completely obscuring the mahouts view forward! In total there were five elephants and they soon head past us to the main square where they are all lined up side by side under a massive canopy. We make our way back down the stairs and follow the throng for the remainder of the evening's fun.

As a visual experience it will take some beating, a lot of what was going on was over our heads, traditional rituals and acts, a whole lot of drumming. As if India is not hot enough the flames from the head of the procession are all still burning bright, adding to the nights heat. If you remember back to our tuk-tuk ride with the lady host at the Sreeragam in Cochin, I mentioned the local wooden temple, describing the grid like frame on the outside of the structure? Now we get to see how that design can be put to spectacular use; hundreds of candles are lit and placed on all the 'shelves,' leaving the temple covered from floor to eaves in flickering light – the overall effect is amazing. We wander around looking at all the light displays before heading back to the car, hopefully what they were telling us about traditional air conditioning methods is true – we are both sweating like the proverbial pigs.

Next morning, we can confirm that our room kept remarkably cool, so traditional techniques did win over modern technology. It is also far quieter than a Mitsubishi wall mounted air conditioning unit. Another amazing breakfast before we say our goodbyes and head back to Kovalum via Trivandrum, for us the Mercury Direct part of the tour is about over...

Amazing experience

Review of Mannaas Veedu

Lovely room attached to the family home - I think there is only about four rooms so it is very exclusive. It was the school holidays & the owners son gave us a tour of the local village up to their rubber tree plantation, pointing out various fruits & trees on the way. Not something we would have considered but we did it as part of the Mercury Direct tour & it was one of the high points of the whole holiday. In the evening we were taken to a local Temple for the festival & again a special experience. Meals are taken in the family home where they serve you up a traditional Kerala meal (both dinner & breakfast) & again the food was amazing. They also have a room to provide ayurveda treatments while you relax there. Cannot recommend highly enough.

Trivandrum was underwhelming, or at least what we see of it. The state capital, and also a major information technology hub – so it is no surprise that amongst all the universities and technology companies scattered around the city it is also home to the Indian Institute of Space Science and Technology! If that is not enough it is also home to the Southern Air Command headquarters of the Indian Air Force and the Thumba Equatorial Rocket Launching Station. While all that may sound grand and exciting, we found it disappointing – all we see was the botanical gardens and the Padmanabhaswamy Temple.

The temple was ok, we have seen better but the setting was pleasant, a long stretch of water alongside and in front, reflecting the buildings on its surface. As we are not practising Hindus the views from the outside are as much as we get to see. The botanical gardens belonged to the Keralan government and was uninspiring, dusty, lacking in care and pretty much a waste of time, sorry about the scathing review... By now we are discovering that the state government has a firm grip on most things in Kerala, we have already mentioned the hotels, now the botanical gardens and when we get to Kovalum we discover the state owned off licenses, the Kerala State Beverages Corporation are the only place for locals to purchase alcohol for their home, or tourists to take to their room.

Kerala citizens may have more government influence (interference?) on their daily life but in many ways, they thrive and benefit. Kerala tops the tables in some important measurements; the highest literacy rate (over 96%) and the highest life expectancy (77.3 years). It is also the second least impoverished state, (Goa is ranked fifth), and if anyone tells you that alcohol is bad for you, more of it is drank in Kerala than in any other Indian state!

Mid-afternoon and we arrive at the Hotel Samudra, another KTDC state owned accommodation. Our first impressions are good, it is what they class as premium beach resort and the buildings and guest rooms are comfortable, almost luxurious. The view from our large room is impressive, amongst the lawned area are some scattered beach bungalows and the swimming pool, beyond that is the sand and sea, the shoreline fringed with swaying palm trees. It is nice to finally get unpacked and have a proper chance to explore the resort and relax.

Our first afternoon is spent by the pool, with time getting on we do not have the inclination to wander far. Disappointingly the pool is not as clean as we like, the water all smells fine but the colour is a little off putting; on the plus side the sunbeds are very comfortable and plentiful. Whilst we haven't got the hotel to ourselves it does not appear to have many guests, but then it is the end of the tourist season. Deja vu strikes, just like on our first night in Kovalum our evening plans go awry when a thunderstorm blows in minutes before we were about to set off for food, we wait a little while but with no sign of it abating we do eat at the on-site restaurant. The food was very good but the atmosphere was soulless, no background noise as there was just a handful of us eating there – not a great start!

Thankfully, the sun was shining next morning, and we were keen to explore Kovalum and find our bearings – which sounds crazy as we had wandered around here only a few days ago! We are used to Goa, one long sandy beach that goes on and on for miles, here there are rocky headlands breaking up the resort into various bays and hiding any landmarks that we would have recognised. Within minutes of setting off we see the lighthouse, so at least know which direction to head in, but first we need to navigate our way across some rough scrubland and onto Grove Beach. On the next rocky outcrop is the Leela Hotel, now that does look posh – a little out of our budget.

If the gleaming white buildings of the Leela is our first distraction it is the local fishermen that soon attract our focus. We are used to seeing fishing boats returning to the beach in Calangute but here they are doing a type of fishing that we have never seen before. Using nets that have floats on they have created an upturned 'U' shape that goes out to sea for perhaps forty metres. At each end of the nets, about thirty metres apart are rows of men who are ready to pull the catch back in, in the upturned horse shoe shaped area are four men creating a whole lot of noise and splashing around, trying to shoo the fish into getting themselves trapped in the confines of the mesh. We stand and watch, fascinated, until they finally start heaving the nets back in towards the beach, gradually closing the area until they are side by side. The fish are then unpicked and put into plastic bowls, little silver ones (the fishes, not the bowls) and the ropes neatly coiled up, ready for the next cast.

With the Leela blocking our coastal walk we keep on heading towards the lighthouse, but along the road until we can access the powdery sand again. Welcome to Kovalum beach the sign says. Here are the beach restaurants that we had discovered on our first day, and it looks like a big event is being prepared for. Flags and posters are proclaiming that tomorrow is the start of India's first national surfing and Stand-Up Paddle boarding (SUP) competition - and the South African cricketer Jonty Rhodes, a keen surfer is there to open it. That is tomorrow sorted, a cold beer in one hand and live sporting entertainment – perfect.

We continue right up to the lighthouse, beyond Hawa Beach; there has been a lot of sitting and travelling over the last few days so it is good to stretch our legs, then at least we can relax around the pool this afternoon without feeling guilty. As we get nearer, we are more impressed by this towering beacon; it is thinner than it looks from a distance, the bright red and white stripes are just how you would draw and colour in as a child. Reading the plaque and it only dates back as far as 1972, prior to that a flame beacon had been lit nightly to warn ships of this treacherous rocky coast. It is also possible to go up the spiral staircase to the top, but unfortunately today its closed...

A lazy afternoon is spent by the pool before we head in for showers and get ourselves dressed to go out and eat, tonight the weather is kind and we end up at the Ocean Breeze. It was a small restaurant with a handful of tables in an outside setting serving fish dishes, having watched todays catch being brought in it seems appropriate. We take advice from the owner of what to try, we know we like fish but at home we are more haddock, salmon or tuna. With our meals ordered we ask if they serve beer, with a smile he heads off and returns with a couple of glasses and a bottle of beer wrapped in newspaper. It seems a ridiculous situation, we are out in plain view with glasses of beer in front of us, sitting under a Kingfisher umbrella but the bottle itself must be kept out of view, or disguised at least! The owner is very personable, probably partly due to the lack of tourists so he has the time to chat.

The meal is that good that we end up eating here every night, the choice of fish dependant on what has failed to outwit the fisherman. As the evenings have gone on our number of beers has also increased, he seems quite happy to sit and talk once we have finished eating, so an after-dinner beer or two has extended our evening. By the final couple of nights, we have even had shorts to finish off – one for the road! The food has been excellent, and it is a shame that there are not more restaurant options in the area, many have already closed for the season. Where our hotel is situated means that for us getting to the main strip of restaurants on Kovalum beach would take either a long walk by a badly lit road, or a taxi. We take the easy option on our doorstep. It is very unusual for us to eat fish night after night, in Goa it is a curry dish every night. On the odd occasion in Calangute that we have gone off-piste and taken a fish option it has never 'wowed' us, maybe we have made poor choices?

With the surf competition in the bay going on today it seems the only place to be, so after another big breakfast we make our way to the flag lined beach. We do not have to watch for very long to see that the standard is not going to be high, third place may well be achieved just by someone being able to stand up. It seems cruel to be laughing; fair play to them for giving it a go, I know for certain that there is no way I could do it, it was just that we were expecting a little more of a spectacle. The star of the show is probably Jonty Rhodes, is it bad form to be the guest of honour, open the competition and then waltz off with the trophy?

Nothing else is spoiling so we sit in one of the beachside restaurants and enjoy a cold beer, uncovered bottle brazenly on show. The surfing does get better, from the announcement over the tannoy there has been a change of category – this must be the one for people who can competently get on the board, and ride a wave. It makes for good viewing as something is constantly happening, the waves are barrelling in one after another – most of them with a surfer riding back towards the shore. My knowledge of surfing is not that great, well almost non-existent - how does the scoring work? Are points awarded for style and technique, or distance? Maybe it's a combination of the two? For us it has kept us amused for a good couple of hours, next stop is to visit the tourist agent who is arranging our driver / guide for a trip down to Kanyakumari, India's equivalent to our Lands' End.

Kanyakumari was known as Cape Comorin during the time of the British Empire. These days it is a small coastal town in Tamil Nadu, most famous for being the southernmost point of the Indian sub-continent and the meeting point of the Indian Ocean, Arabian Sea, and the Bay of Bengal. It is also said to be the only place on earth where you can see the sunrise and sunset from the ocean, we can confirm that you do see both but it is still a bold claim. As well as attracting visitors due to its geographical location it is also a Hindu pilgrimage site, who flock to the Kanyakumari temple on one of the rocky outcrops just off the coast. The temple is dedicated to Kanya Devi, who is considered a virgin goddess who blesses pilgrims and tourists who flock to the town. According to Hindu legend, Kanya Devi, an incarnation of Parvati, was to marry Shiva, but failed to show up on the wedding day. It seems like all must have been forgiven if she has had a temple built in her honour?

Our driver / guide speaks good English and is telling us a lot about where we are heading, it sounds like it is a regular trip for holidaymakers in Kovalum. One piece of information took us completely by surprise; since 2010 a no littering policy alongside a ban on single use plastic and plastic bags has cleaned up the city completely. It claims to be the cleanest city in the whole of India! He is telling us this story as we have brought some crisps and snacks in a thin plastic bag, in Kanyakumari that would be an instant one hundred rupee fine just for having it. Littering carries the same fine for your first offence, caught a second time and it is a thousand. We decant our snacks into our patchwork bag from Goa.

Our hotel is right on the sea front, we have paid for sea views as the sight line across to the Vivekananda Rock Memorial and the Thiruvalluvar statue is supposed to be spectacular. Following our check-in, we are shown up to our room and the guy from reception has us stand back while he pulls back the curtain, revealing the scene as if we were at the theatre. We have to hand it to him though, it was very worthy of the big build up. Not ones for spending longer in hotel rooms than essential we abandon our bags and set off out to explore.

There is a hustle and bustle about this place, but in a good way. It is very much a tourist resort like we have back at home, souvenir sellers, food outlets and boat trip options. The queue for a trip out to sea and a visit to the rocky outcrops runs for far enough, later if time permits for us. We have a rough map of the town from reception so have plenty to be discovering, the Bhagavathy Amman Temple and the Gandhi Memorial Mandapam are the first two on our list, once they have been 'crossed off' there are another couple that we would like to see if we have time. It did not take long to cross off the Ammam Temple, entry for males meant removing your shirt, bare chested entry was one of the conditions – so we gave that a miss. From the outside it is nothing special to look at, although it does date back three thousand years. The story of the temple is very convoluted, and hard to follow – it is one of fifty-two Shakti Pitha, these are the significant shrines and pilgrimage destinations in Shaktism, the goddess-centric denomination in Hinduism. From what we can make out it is another temple where the name Kanya Devi is heavily involved. The names of Gods, Goddesses and Deities, there reincarnations, manifestations and appearance in the form of are just mind blowing, so let us move on...

The Gandhi Memorial is far simpler for us to follow – we know exactly who he is, and following our visit to the museum in Mumbai, we already have a half-decent knowledge of his life and achievements. It is a small attractive building, three stories high with a pair of elongated domes to the front, painted white with light blue trim with the iconic spinning wheel (in orange) from the older Indian flag showing above the entrance door. The central dome is seventy-nine feet tall (twenty-four metres), a deliberate height as that was his age when he was tragically assassinated. The word mandapam translates as pillared hall or pavilion, though we would describe it as slightly grander than that! The reason it is built here, right upon the shores, is because upon his death it is where one of the twelve urns that his ashes were split up between was immersed into the sea. Before immersion members of the public were able to pay their final respects, and this memorial has been built upon that exact spot. The real clever, or poignant feature of this memorial is a small opening in the ceiling of the building. It has been built in such a way that on Gandhi's birthday, the second of October, the rays of the sun light up where the urn was placed as a lasting tribute to him.

Inside the memorial are a few plaques and images, all on black marble with orange trim. We can barely have been in there for more than a minute or two when one of the officials offers us a full escorted tour, and before we know it, he has opened the gates preventing access to the hallowed spot, with the plaque pronouncing 'on this spot were the ashes of Mahatma Gandhi kept on (the) twelfth February 1948 before immersion'. I think he wanted a go with our camera, it is just a shame that all the photographs came out blurred or wonky! The tip dilemma was in our heads, far too often white faces are seen as walking wallets, but this was an official who genuinely wanted to enhance our experience. We went up to the third tier and the views were stunning, an elevated view across to the statue and rock memorial.

Heading back in the direction of our hotel and the queues for the boats show no sign of subsiding, it does not look like we will get out to the islands. We are not too worried as we get a perfectly good view from here on land, it would be safe to say that the statue would be too big anyway to capture on film once you have landed. On one of the rocky outcrops is the Vivekananda Rock Memorial, it was built in 1970 in honour of Swami Vivekananda, who is said to have attained enlightenment on the rock. More myths and legends anyone? It was on this rock that Goddess Kanyakumari performed tapas in devotion of Shiva. Tapas in the Hindu language means acts or penance, nothing to do with the Spanish dish, patatas bravas... Goddess Kanyakumari is the lady who the town takes its name from.

It is the other rocky island that is the more impressive of the two, there is a huge statue stood upon an imposing pedestal. The statue is of Thiruvalluvar, (more commonly known as Valluvar), who was a famous Tamil poet and philosopher. Today his work is considered exceptional, but strangely not much is known about him, or at least not with any certainty. Even the era when he was alive has a nine-hundred-year time frame, anything from 400BC to 500AD seems possible. Never the less his works have influenced a wide range of scholars over the years, and across multiple spheres - ethical, social, political, economic, religious, philosophical and spiritual. He is considered as a great sage, and his literary works a classic of Tamil culture. His statue, including the base is 133 feet tall (nearly forty-one metres), a nod to the 133 chapters of the Thirukkural Couplets. The ninety-five feet statue of Valluvar himself represents the chapters on 'wealth' and 'Pleasure.' The thirty-eight-foot pedestal symbolising the thirty-eight chapters on 'virtue' in the Thirukural. These carefully considered dimensions are there to give the message that wealth and love should be built upon a foundation of solid virtue. Even non-philosophers like us are impressed, very clever of the architects and sculptors who turned the original idea in 1975 into reality, with the grand unveiling on the first day of the new millennium. To be fair, it was 1990 before construction had begun.

It is while we are admiring this statue that we look back to shore on the left and spot the white spires of a more familiar style of church, which after a good trek turns out to be the Our Lady of Ransom Catholic church. It is shockingly white, gleaming in the sun like Greek villas clinging to the hillsides, nothing in India is ever this white! We initially read that it has been there since the sixteenth Century, but then it follows up that the current construction is just under a hundred years old. The white is so bright that we are surprised the smell of paint is not still in the air. We are pleased it caught our attention as getting here took us past a very colourful shoreline, fishing boats of all colours bobbing around in a harbour, or sheltered bay to be more exact. We then navigated a maze of alleyways (with a couple of dead ends), following the spires before the built-up area suddenly opens out to a paved area and this pristine church.

Back on the shoreline we watch the sunset from a purpose-built viewing platform, but in all honesty, it is not the greatest – typically, the early evening cloud has got in first. All that is left for us to do tonight is to get ourselves fed, a night off from the catch of the day. We cannot remember what we ate as our main, or even where, but what does stick in our minds is our first ever taste of gulab jamon – how have we missed this for so long? Super sweet, you can almost feel your teeth rotting as you eat, but wow – delicious.

Next morning, we are about bright and early, even before our breakfast is available. The sunrise is good, but again partial cloud cover has stopped it from being great; the queue for the boat across to the Rock Memorial and statue is already long. A wander around as the tourist shops began to open for another day – Kanyakumari is clean, our guide is right, shops do not hand out plastic bags, purchases are either wrapped in newspaper or in paper bags. What we also notice is that there are waste paper bins everywhere, something that you very rarely see in other parts of the country. There is hope that one day India will become a tidy litter free place?

Our time here is done, all that is left for us to do is get our breakfast, collect our bags as our driver will be collecting us for the return journey. From our TripAdvisor review it sounds that the breakfast was a cracker, another sugar fix ...

Amazing views of India's 'Land End'

Review of Hotel Seaview

Brilliant location, stunning view - when shown to your room they have the curtains drawn & then 'unveil' the view to you, stunning. The room is very large, well equipped. If being picky the bathroom let it down, more of a wet room & a fusty smell! The hotel restaurant is barely large enough, at breakfast it was a struggle to find somewhere to sit - but the choice was brilliant. Try the carrot dish, it is in the fruit & desert sections - genius to make a pudding out of carrots & is truly amazing.

Room tip: Pay the few pounds extra (literally is just 2 or 3) for the better rooms, higher floor & view is well worth it.

On the way back our driver surprises us with one final treat, a place that we had never heard of but had one of the most impressive Hindu temples that we have ever seen. A brief stop in Suchindram gives us a chance to visit the Thanumalayan Temple, built in the gopura style, (that is the pyramid shaped one with amazing figures carved on every available bit of space), it is eleven stories high and forty-four metres tall. The temple is one of the few in the region that combines both Keralan and Tamil style architecture, and it is famous for two reasons; one, the quality of workmanship in stone is unsurpassed and two, the representation of the three central gods of Hinduism in one linga makes it unique in India. It is these three Gods that also give the temple its name - Shiva (Thanu), Vishnu (Maal) and Brahma (Ayan).

Back in the car and within two hours we are sat by the pool at the hotel, our holiday is almost over. We have one more experience to add to the collection, buying alcohol from the Kerala State Beverages Corporation (KSBC), the state governed off license! These shops are nothing like a supermarket or corner shop at home (or in Goa); they are a shop with a counter where you pay for your purchases at one till and then collect them from another hatch. A board with the price list is displayed prominently but you do not have the chance to browse, think Argos but for alcohol. Maybe the football style crush barriers are required at peak times, Kerala is the largest consumer of rum in India after all. Combine that with the brandy and that is ninety-four percent of all KSBC sales accounted for – what we took home, a bottle each of Old Monk and Honey Bee is hardly likely to raise those figures...

We thoroughly enjoyed our visit to Kerala, we booked it very cheaply, knowing that it was the end of the season. Our eating out options could have been better, (though we loved every fish dish we ate), if more restaurants had still been open. Likewise, our hotel was not in the greatest location either – we were fine getting to Kovalum beach in daylight, but come night time that was not possible on foot. Hindsight is a wonderful thing, it didn't stop our fun, we had a brilliant festival experience and see some ~~top class~~ very average surfing! It is very different to Goa in many ways, but that is what we wanted – would we go back, definitely!

Great location views wise but away from main resort

Review of Hotel Samudra KTDC

Lovely landscaped gardens & pool area, hammocks in among the palm trees, lovely view, but a good twenty-minute walk to the main resort area around Lighthouse Beach. Even this walk is only possible in daylight as it starts off with 100 yards or so across an unevenly gravelled stretch of land. The food was good on the night we stayed in the hotel & the breakfasts were plentiful (all buffet style), mix of cereals, Indian options & fresh fruit. Rooms cleaned every day plus a new water bottle and tea / coffee replaced.

Top row: Calangute Beach, Goa; Palace of the Winds, Jaipur

Middle: Taj Mahal, Agra; Mehrangarh Fort, Jodhpur; City Palace, Udaipur

Bottom: Ranakpur Jain Temple and the carvings inside.

Top row: Stone Chariot, Hampi; Elephants in Periyar National Park, Kerala

Middle: Dhobi Ghat, Mumbai

Bottom: Kanyakumari, Tamil Nadu; Kathakali Dancers in Cochin

Top row: Mysore Palace, Karnataka; Wagah Border Ceremony, Punjab

Middle: Golden Temple by night, Amritsar

Bottom: Golden Temple by day Amritsar; Ghats of Varanasi, Uttar Pradesh

November 2013 - Goa and Amritsar

November, and our second visit to India this year. A big bonus is that there had been no visa application to worry about, we had taken out the twelve-month option before we headed to Kerala. After last year's disaster with the twenty-four-hour delay at Manchester we opt to fly out from Gatwick, again opting for a hotel and parking package. The hotel part goes smooth, a very comfortable stay and a nice meal at a nearby pub the night before our departure, perfect. It was one of those deals where you still need to move your car to the parking facilities next morning, rather than leave it at the hotel, but that is no problem. All is going smooth, until the airport transfer bus starts making strange noises on route to the airport, the driver pulls over and tries the best cure known to man, he turns it off and switches it on again. The bus engine starts but as soon as he puts it in gear the same growling noises resurface. It is a minor hitch, with being so close to the airport and in such good time it was not a concern, more a here we go again moment...

Boarded and departed on time, the issue with the coach was the only hiccup of the day. We are on a Thomas Cook package and one of their own planes, not as luxurious as our flight to Kerala but certainly nothing to complain about. Even our transit through Dabolim airport on our arrival into Goa seemed easier, perhaps we just mentally prepare ourselves for it better year on year. For us it is a change of hotel this year, the grandly named Lambana Resort, there will be no shock on arrival as we are not expecting grand, we are almost certain that we have had a drink there in the past – it has a nice bar on the front, more than likely a happy hour had seduced us in.

The room that we are allocated is on the side of the property, but of a very good size. We have a long balcony, but not much of a view – the back of more apartments, but on the plus side we are sheltered from some of the noise from the Calangute to Baga road. Very predictably we have chosen a place to stay at the mid-point of our favourite haunts. For those of you familiar with Calangute we are on the same side of the road as Infantaria, on the left-hand side if you are heading towards Baga. Breakfast is the usual affair, toast! We had never been around the back of the Lambana, and are impressed. The free-form swimming pool is a decent size, not that we do any swimming of note, more just a quick dip now and again for cooling off. The bar is available for drinks, although it is quite a trek, they are missing a trick by not just having a little one in the pool area. Having been up a lot of the night travelling it is good to relax, read until you feel your eyes close and hopefully catch up on a little sleep.

Early afternoon and it is time to eat, Mirabai's where else! Sitting in there and nothing has changed, or at least not décor wise. The Chilli Chicken is disappointing, the chicken is in some kind of coating, rather than just being plain breast – the one redeeming feature is the fiery dried chillies are sticking out the top, a bit like the cow horns in Desperate Dan's pie from the comics. This year's review of the dish though is bang average. It looked the part; my hopes were high - but they have messed with the chicken. At least the bottle of Kingfisher was ice-cold.

From Mirabai's you can work your way down to the beach without having to go back up to the main road, so that is the plan. Rather than walk towards Baga we start to head towards the steps at Calangute, but get accosted by one of the guys from a shack. In all our visits we have never had a beer at this end of the resort, the shack looks busy (always a good sign), the beds comfortable. What impressed us most was that each sunbed had a bowl of water to rinse your feet in, avoiding sand on your mattress, what a great idea. The beer was cold, and we were tired, my eyes drop shut... I am not sure how long I have been asleep for but I have just been startled by a cow! I should say thirsty cow, that bowl of water at the end of my bed has been its focus – whether it nudged me while drinking or was just a sixth sense that it was there alerted me, I do not know. Alison can hardly sit up for laughing...

Showered, and fed (no idea where at), we spend our first evening in Madhu's, and there is no sign of Ricky. Nothing much has changed; the Chef is sat at his usual table on the second row back! We have a quick hello; we will catch up properly on an afternoon visit when its quieter. Friends of ours who we met the year before join us, they have already been here for a few weeks, the joys of retirement! It seems that Ricky has got married to a girl in his village, we will miss him in his Sunderland shirt – the 'new' Ricky has big shoes to fill. Mike and Sylvia are great company, Sylvia always looks immaculate, her hair perfectly in place despite having worn a helmet on the back of the scooter getting here. It is a good night, lots to catch up on and lots to drink – we always seem to get carried away on our first night, we put it down to excitement.

As with our usual Goa fortnights, it is the base for further travel and discovery. This year the Punjab city of Amritsar. It is one of those places that we have wanted to visit ever since we got our taste for travel, but it is not the easiest place to reach with no direct flights from Goa. Amritsar is situated right up in the North-West of India, within touching distance of the Pakistan border and the home of the Wagah Border ceremony, where the gates separating the two countries are theatrically closed at sunset each evening. It is most famous for being the home of the Golden Temple, the premier spiritual shrine and pilgrimage destination for Sikhs across the world. Sadly, the third thing that Amritsar is most remembered for is being the location of an atrocity whilst under British Empire rule.

Valerie is in her usual good form, the same bundle of energy as always. She has arranged our tour as usual, a flight to Delhi and overnight stay there, before catching the morning train from Delhi Junction to Amritsar. We have two nights there, on the first of those we will make the short journey and head to the Wagah Border for the nightly closing ceremony. The following day we have a guided tour around the city and our visit to the Golden Temple, something that we have been really looking forward to since arranging this excursion. Our tour will end that evening, but a driver will collect us from the hotel and run us to the train station next morning, and then another driver will collect us from Delhi Junction and ferry us to the airport... It all sounds good by us. Valerie arranges these types of tours all the time, and her attention to detail and care of her customers is second to none. We always fear delays, the train late arriving into Delhi and we miss our flight back to Goa, Valerie laughs off our concerns, she has every confidence in Indian time-keeping...

Another night in Madhu's, same routine of a Kingfisher beer to start with before a 180ml bottle each of Old Monk and Honey Bee and an ice-cold bottle of Coca Cola between us. If our luck was in the ice bucket would have been available too! Our pick up for the airport is not until late morning so we can enjoy our night to the full, plenty of water before we go to sleep to keep us rehydrated and all will be fine. The usual crowd are in and we get introduced to Ken and Mo, friends of Mike and Sylvia – we get more envious of those who have reached retirement every year, they know how to enjoy themselves - and that does not include spending winter at home in the United Kingdom. It is another great evening and we can see all the plus points. It is like a health resort for pensioners. Evenings can be spent at local markets complete with live music and dancing, days sat in the sun or touring the countryside on their scooters. They tell us how they and some of their friends will have a full health check whilst here, any necessary dental work done, teeth whitening, eyes tested and new glasses purchased etc. All of this is at a fraction of the cost of back home, on the other hand their alcohol intake must be giving their livers a good workout! It certainly opens our eyes to how much fun you can have in your later years, Club 18 – 30 has nothing on this bunch.

No hangovers, and an average breakfast. Now it is a case of loitering around, passing time until the taxi picks us up. Everything runs to schedule and before we know it, we have been deposited at a hotel in Delhi, near to the Delhi Junction railways station ready for the next leg of our journey tomorrow. Delhi is just as smoggy and intimidating as we remember it, we venture as far as a local shop just to get some juice and snacks for the train. Another hotel meal, but another that has left us with no memory of it, so guess it wasn't great but never gave us upset stomachs either.

Delhi Junction station was a shock, although by now it shouldn't be. The usual pattern of stepping over sleeping bodies to make our way to the platform where we needed to be, it was like the streets of Mumbai all over again. Could they all be waiting to catch trains today, or is it just people with nowhere else to put their heads down at night? As much as you know this is life for many in India it is always uncomfortable to see it with your own eyes, it is really shocking. Our train soon picks us up, and just to add to our awkward feeling we are in the first-class compartment. It soon becomes evident that we need not have gone out for snacks yesterday, a breakfast was brought out to us soon after departing the station.

Parathas, yoghurts, a rice dish, milkshakes and a jug of hot water were all placed on our tray, and it was all tasty. Parathas, until the other year had been off my radar, they were a staple component of breakfast options in Kerala and this Indian take of a stuffed pancake is well worth trying if you get the opportunity. It certainly left us full, and the cups of chai were top notch too; all included in the price of our rail fare too. The train rumbled on for just over seven hours, arriving in Amritsar mid-afternoon where we were picked up by a driver to whisk us to our hotel on the outskirts of the city. By the time we had checked into the hotel we could do nothing but wait for our guide for tonight's trip to the Wagah border crossing, a quick freshen up and he will soon be here.

Our guide was a young Sikh chap, knowledgeable and with excellent spoken English. He told us a little bit about Sikhism and some of their traditions, and in doing that gave away what colour pants he was wearing in the process! Guru Gobind Singh was the tenth and final human Sikh Guru and formally installed as the leader of the Sikhs at the age of nine, and it was he who commanded that all Sikhs must wear or carry the five articles of their faith, collectively known as the five K's. These are not just symbols of devotion, collectively they are their identity and show commitment to the Sikh way of life. He tells us that there are three degrees of Sikhism, the Khalsa or 'pure' Sikh who has taken Amrit (been baptised) will have all five on his person. An Amrit Dhari Sikh is working his way up to becoming a fully-fledged Khalsa, while a Sikh who has not taken Amrit but follows the teachings of the Sri Guru Granth Sahib is called a Sahaj Dhari Sikh. We are hoping that there is no test at the end...

Our travel guru (very appropriate), tells us that he is a Khalsa Sikh, and that in true Sikh tradition if they draw their kirpan in anger, they must be prepared to use it. If you are wondering what a kirpan is, that is a dagger, one of the five K's. Thankfully for us Sikh's are peace loving people, and in carrying that dagger it symbolises their duty to come to the defence of those in peril. The kirpan is kept razor sharp but is only allowed to be used in the act of self-defence, a true Sikh cannot turn a blind eye to injustice - carrying that weapon represents bravery and standing up for the weak and innocent, even if that means putting yourself in danger. It sounds like we have our own personal bodyguard for this tour.

The other four Ks are kesh, kangha, kara and kachera. Kesh is their term for the uncut or long hair that we recognise as part of their identity. They consider hair as an indispensable part of the human body; a Sikh never cuts or trims any hair as a symbol of respect for the perfection of God's creation. The turban itself is worn as a spiritual crown, a constant reminder that they are sitting on the throne of consciousness and are committed to living according to Sikh principles. With all that hair they need a kangha, a wooden comb that should be used twice a day. Combing their hair is a constant reminder that their lives should be kept tidy, but also a symbol of that what God has given you should be nurtured and maintained with grace. The Kara is simply an iron bracelet that should be worn at all times, and a constant reminder that what you do with your hands has to be in keeping with the advice given by the Guru. The circle of the bracelet is also to symbolise the permanent bonding to the Sikh community. Finally, the kachera, baggy boxer short style white undergarments... The constant wearing represents their duty to be permanently ready for action, and some take that instruction to such an extreme that when changing them they will remove one leg from the ones heading to the wash basket, and then put that 'undressed' leg into the clean pair before removing the second leg from the dirty pair. That is dedication.

He is imparting all this knowledge upon us on as we head to the lowering of the flag's ceremony at Wagah, he also has time to point out some of the strange additions to the roofs of local houses. In the Punjab region there has developed a strange tradition of showing off what your job is, especially amongst the wealthy. It seems that many families in the Punjab work overseas, or maybe their children have done well and are earning a good living in the UK, Canada, Australia or the Middle East. The planes on the rooftops may represent the perceived jet set lifestyle, giant eagles are more a generic sign of wealth, a pair of lions, even the national symbol of a peacock – they would make for a brilliant game of I Spy...

At the border crossing, passports in hand we are ushered through the gates for the VIP's, basically international visitors and tourists. With our documents having been checked we make our way onto the terracing with simple seating but with a prime view of the gates. Continuing the football theme, as that is the best way that I can think of to describe the atmosphere, we are in the equivalent of the family stand. The quieter area, interested onlookers without a dog in the fight to the incredible charade that is starting to be played out in front of us. To our right is the partisan Indian crowd, a big picture of Gandhi looking down on proceedings. To the left on the other side of the wall, but in sight through the gate is the Pakistan supporters, and their father-figure portrait of Jinnah. Music is being pumped through the tannoy system, lots of dancing and chanting – 'Hindustan!' from our side, 'Pakistan!' echoing back from the other side of the gate. This goes on for a good half hour, we even recognise some of the music from the soundtrack of Slumdog Millionaire. With the crowd being built up into a frenzy more soldiers are coming into view, on 'our' side the Indian flag is proudly being ran up and down in front of the baying, cheering crowd. Bollywood tunes take over from Slumdog, and the ladies start showing off their best dance moves, older children still in school uniform adding to the huge numbers - this is pure theatre...

As the sun drops everyone is ushered off the 'dance floor' and it is turned back into a parade square. It is now time for the big match, India Border Security Force versus Pakistan Rangers (that is their genuine name). By now we have six moustachioed soldiers in full dress; black boots, white under-trousers with stirrups around the foot and a khaki coloured trouser and shirt combination. They look resplendent with gold braiding, red sashes and red ice-cream wafer headwear, trimmed with four thin gold stripes. Across the other side of the gate are their Pakistani counterparts, a full black uniform with white trim around the shoulders and chest. A red cummerbund around the waist and further red trim on a black ice-cream wafer hat. The scene is set, kick off, or should that be high-kick off is fast approaching.

Posturing, gesticulating and staring are the opening gambit. Twiddling of the moustache, is that nerves or part of the routine? And then they are off, a blur of high kicking, heel turns, foot stamping - its bizarre marching meets Olympic gymnastics meets Strictly Come Dancing. There is a definite comedy element to the procedure, think Monty Python's Ministry of Silly Walks sketch, but done in uniform, and between two countries with nuclear weapons, and with not a lot of love between them at times... Back and forth they go, alternating between being almost balletic at times, who can raise their foot and point their toes the highest, but then swiftly replaced with who can do the most aggressive, loudest stamp. All too soon the spectacle is over, the freestyle, or maybe semi-choreographed march-off is put to one side for the more symbolic and diplomatic part of the performance.

With the sun about to disappear for the day the respective national flags are lowered simultaneously. The flags are removed and folded, before the ceremony is rounded off with a brusque handshake between the soldiers from either side, followed by the closing of the gates with a firm slam. This whole ceremony has taken place every day since 1959 at what was once the only road link between the two countries. These days the soldiers are trained especially for this auspicious daily event, and can even earn bonuses for displaying a quality moustache! The crowds continue to flock here night after night, with numbers often reaching the twenty-thousand plus mark... and we can see why, without doubt that is one of the best, most fun and maddest experiences we have ever had.

Breakfast, and we had been tipped off by Valerie that Amritsar is famous for one particular breakfast dishes, Amritsari kulcha – and our hotel was serving it! Amritsari kulcha, wow! Simple but so tasty, it is a soft bread but stuffed with spiced mash potato or cottage cheese and then baked to a golden crisp in the tandoor. That beats toast, we could have had that if we wanted, and leaves you very full – which is good as we have a big day ahead of us.

With the same guide as yesterday, we are taken into Amritsar city, and the first stop for us is at the Jallianwala Bagh, infamous for the Amritsar massacre on what was one of the darkest days of British Empire rule. Bagh is the Indian name for a walled garden, or what we might call a courtyard, one entrance in and no other way out. Its name, Jallianwala Bagh translates as the garden of the Jallah-man, which suggests that with its well for a constant supply of water it was once a green and flowering oasis, popular as a park for those visiting the nearby Golden temple. In 1919 it was just a dried-out wasteland, albeit a seven-acre plot. These days it is home to a park, a historic garden and a memorial to all of those murdered within its grounds. Access is still though the original narrow passageway, once you get inside the bullet ridden walls are still there, as is the well where many leapt to their deaths. An art gallery and museum tell the full grim story of that shocking day.

In 1919 the Rowlatt Act was enforced in India to limit civil liberties, Britain was short-staffed, World War One and a flu pandemic had taken its toll both financially and in manpower. Mahatma Gandhi was emerging as an increasingly charismatic leader, encouraging civil disobedience and political unrest. On the 13th April 1919 Amritsar was in lockdown, mass gatherings were not allowed, groups of four were the maximum but a large peaceful crowd had gathered at the Jallianwala Bagh to protest against the Rowlatt Act. The temporary Brigadier General Reginald Dyer was in charge, and feared what could happen next – his troops were vastly outnumbered. From his own testimony it is revealed that the crowd was not given any warning to disperse, which makes what he did next even more incredible.

Dyer arrived at the Bagh with a group of fifty troops, all carrying Lee–Enfield .303 bolt-action rifles. The troops were a mix of Gurkhas and Sikhs, Dyer may have specifically chosen troops from those ethnic groups due to their proven loyalty to the British. The two armoured cars armed with machine guns (thankfully) could not fit through the narrow entrances. On Dyer's order the troops began shooting into the densest sections of the crowd, the firing is said to have continued for approximately ten minutes. Unarmed civilians - men, women, young and old were killed. A cease-fire was only ordered when ammunition supplies were almost exhausted.

At the subsequent investigation Dyer openly admitted that his actions were not to disperse the meeting but to punish the Indians for disobedience. Dyer went on to say "I think it quite possible that I could have dispersed the crowd without firing, but they would have come back again and laughed, and I would have made, what I consider, a fool of myself". Exact figures of dead and casualties from that day are disputed, British figures suggest nearly four hundred dead and up to fifteen hundred wounded, the Indian National Congress suggests around thousand were killed, whilst others suggest it was nearer fifteen hundred deaths.

Looking around the gardens now it is hard to take in the horrors that these walls have witnessed. The well is now known as the Martyrs Well, the plaque says that one hundred and twenty bodies were recovered from its depths, choosing to jump and drown rather than being shot. One of the walls has thirty-six bullet holes circled in white paint, telling the story of how 1,650 rounds were fired into a peaceful crowd. Further memorials are placed around the grounds and the museum includes several paintings depicting scenes from that day. After the fun and joy of last night this has brought us right back down to earth with a bump.

We exit the gateway and are back on the main road, just a short walk from the Golden Temple. I am taken by surprise when told that I will have to wear a head covering, Alison was well prepared and has a scarf with her, many places in India insist on women covering their heads. Getting a headscarf is no problem, street vendors all sell them for an exceedingly small price, and with a bit of help to put it on I am suitably dressed... in the brightest of orange. With our shoes handed over, bare footed we join the small queue to walk through the foot baths, before entering the holiest site of the Sikh religion.

As we walk out into the quadrant, the lake spread before us and the sun shining off the roof of the Golden Temple we are in awe, completely blown away. It was smaller than we had imagined, but the vibrant colour, and its reflection in the water was just stunning. The atmosphere inside was instantly noticeable, one of calm, readings (more melodic singing or chanting really), from the Sikh book of prayer, so different from the hustle and bustle of the streets and alleys outside. Without doubt this is the single most beautiful building that we have ever seen, on the day we were lost for words, and looking through the photographs today it still has the same effect. Our guide for the day is certainly living up to his duties, 'whenever he meets a traveller or a pilgrim from a foreign country, he must serve him devotedly.' He starts off by telling us how he contributes ten percent of all his earnings for the welfare of the community, and in addition to that he helps with his hands, physical work or just serving and helping the less fortunate.

The four buildings around the side of the man-made lake symbolises their belief in equality. The entire complex is all encompassing, regardless of colour, caste, religion, gender or sexuality – everyone is welcome. The architecture of the four sides surrounding the water represent different corners of the globe; Arabesque, Gothic, Muslim and of course Indian – and each of these four sides also has an entrance, echoing the sentiment of inclusivity. Everything is immaculate, the white buildings with their decorative gold trim shimmering against the blue sky are perfect. The lake, or the Holy tank is where the city takes its name from 'Amrit' means the nectar of immortality and 'Sar' means pond - hence the name. Whilst it might be known across the world as the Golden Temple these days, most Sikhs still refer to it as Harmandir Sahib, meaning God's Temple.

The foundations of the temple go right back to 1577, when the man-made pool on the site of the temple was dug out under the instruction of the fourth Sikh Guru, Guru Ram Das. By 1604, Guru Arjan Dev (the fifth Sikh Guru) was able to place a copy of the Adi Granth, the central holy religious scripture of Sikhism in the Harmandir Sahib. The Temple was rebuilt by the Sikhs repeatedly over the next two centuries, it was a constant target for destruction by first the Mughal Empire and then later by invading Afghan armies from the north. This situation persisted for nearly two hundred years, right up until Maharaja Ranjit Singh finally united the whole Punjab region and became the first Maharaja of the Sikh Empire. In 1802, twenty-two-year-old Ranjit Singh paid homage at the ruins of the Harmandir Sahib Temple, following the latest attack by the Afghan army, and announced that he would renovate and rebuild it with marble and gold. The Temple was rebuilt by 1809, a structure of marble and copper and by 1830 it had been overlaid with gold leaf, and recognisable as the Golden Temple that we know today.

Sadly, that is not the complete story, or the end of conflict at this holy place, in early June 1984 Indias own military units under orders from Prime Minister Indira Gandhi were involved in an eight-day battle to remove militant Sikh Jarnail Singh Bhindranwale and his followers from the temple complex. After an initial stand-off three days of intense fighting ensued that left the army with eighty-three dead and 249 injured, 1,592 militants were apprehended in the military operation. Less than five months after the operation, on the thirty-first of October 1984, Indira Gandhi was assassinated in an act of revenge by her two Sikh bodyguards.

The Golden Temple itself is set a little below ground level, so as you take the walkway leading to it you head down a small set of stairs that take you lower than the concourse that surrounds the lake. The significance, or symbolism of it is a reminder to stay humble, you must go down to reach the temple of God. The architecture of the Golden Temple itself is described as a mixture of the Indo-Islamic Mughal and the Hindu Rajput architecture... why not just say its unique? With no photography allowed inside the actual temple itself we have no internal pictures, though we do remember it being even 'blingier' and shinier on the inside than on the out. Reading more about it all the domes, inner walls and the door panels exhibit gold work. Special designs have also been added to the copper sheets prior to them being covered with gold leaves. Maharaja Ranjit Singh was the one who first covered the domes and roof in gold back in 1830, twenty-four carat gold as well, no expense spared. Records suggest that he used 162 kilogrammes of gold. In the 1990s it was renovated and a further five hundred kilogrammes of gold were added... the price of gold today, roughly fifty thousand pounds per kilo...

If the Golden Temple is the cherry on the cake, the buildings on each side of the lake are very impressive icing. If you are walking the causeway towards the Temple itself the Akal Takht building is standing right behind you. It is probably the most impressive of the four. Its name Akal Takht means 'Throne of the Timeless (God).' The Sikh tradition has five Takhts, all of which are major pilgrimage sites in Sikhism, the Akal Takht in the Golden Temple complex is the highest of them all. It is a four- or five-tiered building, in white but topped with gold domes. To the left of the building are two flag poles, each with orange flags hanging, while the balcony has a further pair.

The Ramgarhia Bunga has two towering red sandstone minarets, the only deviation away from the colour white. These were built in the eighteenth century, the only remaining part from the days of Afghan attacks and temple demolitions. Muslim in style they were there primarily for defence purposes, watchtowers for sentinels to look out for any military raid approaching the temple. Amritsar used to have lots of them, but most of the other towers around the city were demolished during the British colonial era. The Ramgarhia Bunga remains as a symbol of the Ramgarhia Sikh community's identity, and as a lasting monument to their historic sacrifices and contribution to defending the Golden Temple.

The Clock Tower did not exist in the original version of the temple, what stood here was a building, now appropriately called the 'Lost Palace.' Another piece of history destroyed by the British, despite opposition from the Sikh community. In its place, the clock tower was added, designed by John Gordon in a Gothic cathedral style in red bricks. The twelve-year build (1862 to 1874) only stood for about seventy years before it was demolished by the Sikh community. In its place, a new design was constructed, keeping more in harmony with the rest of the Temple. There is still a clock, but it also houses a museum, and the red brickwork has long gone, replaced with a lovely white finish.

Having watched many programmes on the Golden Temple we were about to visit what has been covered on nearly all of them, not a place of beauty or calm but the chaos and noise of the world's largest community kitchen. Langar, serving your community. The langar (Community Kitchen) at the Golden Temple serves a massive number of vegetarian meals up to one hundred thousand a day! On holidays or religious occasions, that number often doubles – Christmas dinner when you cook for twelve is enough to bring on palpitations. Women play a key role in the preparation of meals; children help in the serving of food and everyone waits their turn and sit together, eating in a community situation. This plays a great part in upholding the virtue of sameness of all human beings; no one gets special treatment, jumps the queue or has a special table. Many a royal and world leader have waited their turn here.

Everyone is welcome to share the langar; no one is ever turned away, local or tourist. With no outside caterers, all the preparation, cooking and the washing-up is done by volunteers. My (shamefully small) contribution was a stir of a massive curry pot... The kitchens are fascinating places, watching the ladies make chapattis by the thousand is something to behold. Parts of the process are automated, or assisted by machinery but there is still a lot of work to do by hand, but equally there are lots of hands who are doing the volunteering. The dozens of racks containing the metal plates are huge, think bath tub size – and each must hold thousands, I am coming out in a cold sweat, a dishwashing nightmare. As you can imagine the food hall is colossus, the ceiling fans are whirring away and wall mounted ones pointing downwards, oscillating so everyone would get a cool fix. When we look in few are eating, but in a way that helps us to get a good idea of the process. The floor is tiled in such a way that you know where to sit, patterned tiles are for sitting on leaving enough space for the sewadar, (the person serving), to wander down the aisle to dish out the food. When this place is full the din must be ear shattering, metal plates are notoriously noisy but thinking about it there is no cutlery, everything will be eaten with your right hand.

As we leave the community kitchen our guide points out a special view, the Golden Temple is perfectly framed through the arches of the Ath Sath Tirath (difficult to say!). Not only that, in the foreground of our vision is silver and gold tinsel, hanging down above our heads - I know I have said it before but this place is truly magical. We walk through the Ath Sath Tirath, (it is also difficult to type), to the lake and it looks like its bath time. It is no coincidence that the bathers are here, the story has it that bathing under this ber tree is the exact place where a Sikh was cured of his leprosy after taking a dip. This tree (a ber tree bears a plum type fruit) has ever since been known by the title of 'suffering remover'. If that isn't good enough this exact spot, under the tree by the Ath Sath Tirath is the equivalent to making sixty-eight pilgrimages.

We have one final walk around the whole complex, the chanting and readings are constantly changing – some are like readings whilst others are more melodic, we wouldn't say they are being sung but there soothing nonetheless. We are stopped on a regular basis, Sikh pilgrims who want to shake our hand, welcome us, and have our photographs taken with them. As our guide initially pointed out, one of their Sikh duties is to serve foreign visitors, if no serving is to be done then a warm welcome is the next best thing they can offer. With the tour over our guide asks if we have any further questions, and it is not often I have one... With the bright orange flags and the amount of orange turbans bobbing around the complex there must be some significance in that colour, our guide explains that it represents courage and wisdom.

It is time to say our goodbyes, but rather than be returned to the hotel we want to stay in the city itself and visit the Golden temple again this evening at dusk. Our guide is delighted that we want to return, promises us that it will be a truly special experience and advises us of where we can arrange a taxi back to our hotel from. When it comes to tipping, he will not accept, or he can't accept, it is that word 'duty' again. We are more than happy to make a bigger donation at the official office in the Temple instead – entry is completely free, even the looking after of your shoes is complimentary... and we are going to return this evening.

In the streets outside we find a small café selling chai, the big frothing pot is being stirred by a saucepan attached to the end of a stick, the pot does not look the cleanest, congealed and stained but that will all add to the flavour! He pours from the big pot into a large teapot, first from almost touching distance between the two vessels but by the time he finishes it is from a great height, I am impressed with his accuracy. The large teapot is then decanted into a smaller one, again in a very showy manner (think cocktail waiter, but without the spinning bottles), before finally being served too us in glass tumblers. It was well worth the wait, ten rupees for a cup of chai with a front row seat to watch his wizardry. Back home tea bags and kettles take all the fun out of making a cuppa! It is these little experiences on the streets that stick in the memory, who cares if his equipment might not have passed UK hygiene standards; this is India - if its good enough for the locals then why not for us?

Our evening meal is a little more fraught, but all turns out well. Amritsar is full of restaurants with the word 'kulcha' in their name, it is the local dish and its available everywhere. It seems that it can be eaten any time of the day too, we have already had it for breakfast today - late-afternoon and they are still being served. We sit in a small restaurant and a young Sikh, in his early to mid-twenties, asks us where we are from? As soon as we say from England, he is straight onto the Jallianwala Bagh massacre – I would not say he was aggressive but it certainly made us feel uncomfortable. We were obviously very apologetic, of course it should never have happened and we explain that having visited the site of the massacre we felt ashamed of not only that but much of what Britain had done in its colonial past. What had started as an awkward situation ended up amicably, in fact better than that, he came over and helped us out with his recommendations on the menu. We obviously liked it ...

Excellent!

With great local advice we tried one of each kind of kulcha (aloo, mix, dal and paneer) and were unable to pick a clear winner. All so very good! Hot, fresh and just the right level of spice for us, the chutney side dish to dip was excellent...
We also had their lassi which we loved. This was by far one of the best meals of our trip.

We got back to the Golden Temple just before dusk, completed another lap and then just sat for the next hour or so, as the sun dipped behind the buildings and darkness fell. All the time the soothing readings from the Sikh holy book, the Guru Granth Sahib were being piped around the temple. The gold of the roof subtlety changed colour as the lights around the place come on. Visiting by night was the right decision, and elevated this enchanting place into a different league of anything we have ever seen before.

So far today we have had a right mix of experiences, this morning was all about a story of unimaginable brutality, followed up with a treat not just for the eyes but also the heart. The warmth that we have been shown, not only by our guide but also by so many other Sikhs in the temple has made us feel so welcome, it really does restore faith in humanity. If that sounds very sentimental then the rest of the day (and night) turns into comedy...

All that is left for us to do is make our way back to the hotel, what could be easier? We have the card from the hotel reception, so we know that we are staying at the HK Clarks Inn, a full address too '14 B - Block District Shopping Complex Ranjit Avenue, Amritsar'. The problem is that it is one of the few places open on what looks like a new development; none of the taxi drivers are familiar with where it is, a look at the card and a shake of the head. We must try six or seven, same response. There is no need to panic as the worst-case scenario is for us to call the hotel and for them to arrange our collection. An older guy, at a guess sixty plus, comes over having seen our predicament, and he knows where it is, and beckons us over to a tuk-tuk driver. They chat between themselves, pointing and motioning with his hands – hopefully giving directions, explaining to the driver where it is, but it is still a no. Finally, the older guy takes us over to his cycle rickshaw and points to the seats, for us to climb aboard.

When I suggested he might be sixty, I could just have easily said seventy – with the upmost respect to him, it is a tougher life in India than what we have, ageing people can be difficult at the best of times. There was nothing of him, he was very thin and wiry - but no doubt deceptively powerful, cycling passengers around all day requires a lot of strength. Navigating his way through the city centre was no problem to him at all, everything was going smooth; he was no Chris Hoy but it was a steady pace. Or at least it was until we approached the flyover by the railway station, the pace got slower, he started standing on the pedals as the going got tougher... I tapped him on the shoulder and motioned a walking movement, suggesting we get out for this bit and walk, he shook his head, no! It was not many more metres before he relented, so we got out while he remained seated and starting helping him out by pushing from behind.

Once we had reached the brow of the bridge, we clamber back aboard, it is a nice easy freewheel down the other side while this poor man gets his breath back. We were not concerned for our safety, but the longer he cycled for we began to wonder if he knew where he was going. Nothing was looking familiar to us, but then again, we had been chatting with our guide, barely paying attention to the outer parts of the city. Eventually our anxiety was eased, Alison recognised a shop that she had seen earlier this morning and within minutes we pulled up into the hotel car park. I have no recollection of exactly what price had been agreed, (my memory says fifty rupees), but do know that it had seemed ridiculously cheap compared to a five-minute tuk-tuk ride in Goa; we paid him and gave him a tip of the same amount, hats off to him - he had dug us out of a hole!

Google maps says the distance is a little over five kilometres by car, it also says it is impossible by bike... so maybe even Google took that steep flyover into account and dismissed cycling ...

Chuckling to ourselves, we head up to our room. What a day, and what an adventure to round it off with! We watch some television, no doubt random channels, anything in English language before turning out the lights for a good night's sleep. Tomorrow morning we have an early pick up, our train for Delhi departs just before eight. We do not seem to have been in bed for long when a loud drumming begins, the noise is getting louder and louder so we look out the windows. Coming up the street is a band of five or six drummers, all wearing bright colours and traditional outfits ... We look on for a minute or two and then they disappear out of sight, to attend a function in our hotel! Any plans for an early night are dismissed; thump, thump, thump of the drums goes on, and on, and on. We have no idea what time we finally got to sleep, but the beep of the alarm was a shock to the system. A quick wash and teeth clean, double check we have not left anything behind before leaving the room and wait for the lift. With perfect comedy timing, the lift doors open, there is no room for us to get in... four men, complete with their offending drum kits are looking back out at us! We get the next lift down and caught up with them in reception, laughing at how they had kept us awake. It turns out there had been a wedding party in one of the function rooms, and Indian weddings would not be the same without a lot a bit of drumming.

The journey back to Goa went exactly as planned, Valerie (as always) was right – we worry too much. Alison slept for almost all of the seven-hour train journey, the full stomach from breakfast and the rocking motion of a train when you are already tired is almost hypnotic. A taxi ferried us from Delhi Junction railway station to Delhi airport where we ate a Kentucky Fried Chicken before boarding our SpiceJet flight home.

As usual the rest of the holiday passes in a blur, our days starting around 9 a.m., alternating between pool and beach, an explore of the town or a walk to Baga. Our hunger varies, but a reluctance to miss an opportunity to eat Indian food is never turned down. Lunches could be taken at the Rovers Return, or snacks from Infantaria, samosas from by the Red Lion. Many days it could be two of them options, that makes us sound greedy! Carvalho's bar and restaurant has been good this year and we have had two particularly good meals at Krishna's, diagonally opposite our accommodation at the Lambana. If you walk through the main restaurant on the roadside, past the open plan kitchen, then if you are lucky there are a handful of tables in a small garden / courtyard setting. Rasoi's Pure Veg restaurant serves decent food, and despite its name there are plenty of meat dishes on the menu. s downhill?

Evenings are always finished off in Madhu's and we even attend a fiftieth birthday party there. Chef, a constant patron, be that afternoon or evening was the person celebrating, a good buffet style spread was laid out and it was an enjoyable evening. We often have a chat with him, usually in the afternoon when the place is quieter. We have watched him play backgammon many a time, not a game that we understand but that is his favourite and a sure way to keep him quiet. He is an interesting guy to talk too, but not everyone's cup of tea! He grew up in Mumbai, is very knowledgeable and good company to share a drink or two with, but can at times be blunt. Oh, and he is a chef.

We remember the Lambana as being an enjoyable stay, the mini bar had eluded our memories though, (posher than we recall), and from our review we had obviously enjoyed it at the time too...

Friendly Staff, Central Location, Nice Rooms

Review of Lambana Resort

Very pleased with our stay here, large room, air conditioned, coffee making facilities, reasonably priced mini bar. Pool area in sun all of the day, plentiful sun beds & very clean. Side rooms are larger than the standard rooms (although no view to get excited about). Rooms at the rear overlook the pool & would be a lot quieter than the rooms at the front that overlook the main road - though that is free entertainment!

Room tip: Pool rooms for quietness, side rooms for size. There is no lift in the hotel.

On our return home the planning for our next visit would begin, only there may be one change this year. The day before we were due to leave Valerie asked us if we had ever considered booking the flight and accommodation separately? It is not something that we had ever contemplated, but we were open to the idea of it, especially if flight times or the departure airport suited us better – neither Gatwick and Manchester were close by. With that in mind she mentioned a couple of options of where we could stay, so we would have the opportunity to look at them before we departed, the Chalston Beach Resort and the Casa Aleixo...

November 2014 - Goa, Bangalore and Mysore

Bonus number one was our flight, Qatar Airways via Doha, departing from Heathrow. What turned out to be bonus number two was our choice of place to stay, the Casa Aleixo in Calangute, a stunning traditional Portuguese villa with the kindest of hosts.

In April last year we had enjoyed our first ever flight with Emirates, so we knew a little more of what to expect from one of the world's top airlines, Qatar did not disappoint. We thought for comfort, the complimentary meal and drinks service plus the in-flight entertainment was every bit as good. With the stopover time in Doha being under ninety minutes it was just a case of stretching your legs on the hike around the airport and getting back on the second plane, there was no time wasted hanging around. It also made financial sense, when we weighed up the (slightly) more convenient departure airport, cost of the flight and arranging our own accommodation. Even considering our taxi transfers (arranged through our host) we were still actually in pocket.

The flight out of Heathrow was luxury; spacious seats, choice of meals and a generous drinks service. By the time we arrived in Doha we were already aware of what gate our next flight was due to depart from, and with the massive signage in the brand-new airport there was little chance of losing your way. The centre piece of the airport was a giant bear of some kind, it reminded us a little of Pudsey, the Children in Need character. We got through security and hand baggage checks in good time and if we got sat down at the gate before boarding it would not have been for more than twenty minutes. The Doha to Goa leg was not as comfortable, it was a smaller plane and the bulk of the passengers were Indians returning home, laden with enormous amounts of cabin luggage! If that was a negative it was more than made up for when we reached immigration, rather than a Thomas Cook or Thomson flight load of tourists there might have only been twenty or thirty of us who had to go through the visa checks – it was the quickest we have ever passed through passport control by a long, long way!

As with nearly all flights into Dabolim it was the middle of the night but the taxi driver was already waiting for us, and in record time we were heading to Calangute. On our last visit the previous year we had looked at both the Chalston and Casa Aleixo, the two places Valerie had recommended. The

Chalston was very nice, but far more expensive than what we were looking to pay, our style of travel is budget, clean and simple accommodation, and the Casa Aleixo was perfect for us. Our driver dropped us off and took our cases to the door, introducing us to some young lad who showed us up to our room. The first thing that grabbed our attention was the vivid colours of the bedding...

Next morning a tap on the door and it was the same young lad who showed us into the main house last night. Today he leads us into another room in the villa for our breakfast; tea and toast with a wide selection of fruit, which changed day by day was the morning fare here. Whilst we were having breakfast our host, Mr Wilfred, came for a chat – it was good to finally put a face to the email conversations that we had around the time of making the booking. He is a really nice guy, very well-travelled himself through business and leisure, and it sounds like he has his finger in many pies business wide even now. Having finished our meal, (and being offered more), he shows us around the facilities that are available to us. There is a balcony overlooking the garden and pool that is for the guests use, and then he walks us down the garden to the pool itself, two sunbeds are out already laid out for us. Mr Wilfred points out the room by it, that is where his staff live and sleep, they will provide us with beach towels and cold beers whenever we like. We have landed on our feet here!

Our morning is spent lazing around the pool, it is small yet big enough to swim around in laps, and more than adequate just to splash around in and cool off. Our first beer of the holiday is also taken, the only problem being that they seem to think that I look like an extra strong Kingfisher drinker, too many of them and I will be fast asleep. The garden is well manicured, the lawns and flowers attracting plenty of wildlife – in the middle of the lawn is a well, and at some point during our stay Mr Wilfred shows us the grooves in the stone caused by wear from the chain pulling up the bucket over the years. Our first thought was that it had been purely ornamental, but no, in the past it had been functional and used by both the house and his neighbours.

By midday we are itching to get our first curry, and of course it has to be at Mirabai's. It is just a short walk away and the owner instantly recognises us and gives us a friendly welcome. The Chilli Chicken dish was still on the menu and it was good, different again from the previous year. Thankfully, the nasty coated chicken from last year has gone, but it is still not as spice laden or intense as our very first one. I am now quite worried that opening meal of our first ever visit is never to be matched, or maybe I have elevated it so high over the years that nothing will ever compare. One custom observed and its onto Madhu's for an afternoon beer, and once again its handshakes all around – the local business people have an unbelievable knack for remembering faces.

Wandering further down the road we take a right turn at the Redondo's roundabout and head down the aptly named Beach Road, everything looks familiar, an extra tattooist or two have opened in the shopping arcades close to the beach. The names we remember from the beach shacks all seem to be there, and we stretch our legs with a walk all the way up to Baga and back, it is good to feel the sand between your toes and we even get our feet wet once we have passed the jet skis, parasailing etc stalls. On our walk back to the Casa Aleixo, (and timed to perfection), we drop in for fresh samosas by the Red Lion, but have them wrapped in newspaper – there is a balcony for us to try out, see if they eat as well with a cup of tea as a cold beer.

It is always good to catch up with Valerie again, email contact is never quite the same. Once again, our out of state jaunt has been arranged by her and we need to pay the balance! The full itinerary looks good, it has deliberately been planned to take in the weekend so that we see Mysore at its finest. When we first started exploring India, we were always nervous, fearing the worst, lost and abandoned in a city of millions. These days we are far more relaxed, and much of that is down to Valerie; she is in telephone contact with the drivers and guides, and often gives them a call to speak to us, checking in that all is well. After a good chinwag we leave her shop, she is a busy lady so we do not want to divert her attention for too long... she can talk for hours!

The next day or two follow similar patterns, a full day on the beach and lunch at the Rovers Return, alternated with a day spent around the pool. With us being the only guests at the Casa Aleixo it is like having your own private villa, complete with pool and beer waiter. Mr Wilfred is the consummate host, checking in that we are happy with everything, chatting to us daily before heading off back to the house or out in the car. We ask him where we can leave our bags whilst we head off to Bangalore and Mysore for three nights, he is quite happy for us to just leave everything in the room, despite us not paying him for those nights that we are away.

The day of our flight to Bangalore arrives, the by now familiar route to Dabolim airport. The domestic flight procedure is so much easier, for one domestic flights head in and out at sociable hours. The queues of Immigration Control are not required either, it is a painless transit, although being in India they do like to check everything multiple times. Internal flights are always different to anywhere else in the world too, the job of a cabin steward is almost impossible. We have taken internal flights in Thailand, Cambodia and Vietnam, they all run like clockwork, people turn off their phones as instructed, sit down for take-off, obey seatbelts signs etc. Without exaggeration we have been on internal flights in India where the plane is taxiing down the runway and people are stood up, rummaging around in the overhead storage. They were probably still chatting on their mobile phone too...

Bangalore was just for an overnight stay, it happens to be the city with the nearest airport to Mysore; onward travel would continue in the morning, another four hours by road. Our driver collects us from the airport and takes us to the hotel, Bangalore is a busy place, but without that permanent smog that we found in Delhi. We will not be venturing too far this evening, there is no charm around the streets where our hotel is based, more main roads and shopping precincts – quite a modern city compared to others that we have visited. Our hotel is functional, key card operated doors and a bathroom you wish you could take home, beautifully tiled and shiny... but all a bit lacking of character.

There is not much either of us can remember about our stay here, not surprising as we arrived at dusk and only walked half a mile in each direction from the hotel, just to see what there is to see! I did buy a sweatshirt from a street vendor, something about it grabbed my attention and the cost was so minimal that I had to have it. First time it was washed it shrunk, not a little – if our two-year-old Grandson had been born it would have fitted him. That sweatshirt went from being a bargain to very expensive, I only ever got one wear out of it! The second memory is the food, or more where we ate. No idea what the place was called but it was across the road from our hotel, and you had to go up some stairs. All it served was thali's, with a choice of veg or non-veg.

Thali is the name of the plate, the metal dish or tray, sometimes with sunken out partitions to keep the various foods separate on it. What is served up on it can vary from region to region, but traditionally you would expect to have a grain in some form, rice (if you are in the south of the country) or flatbread if you are in the north. These are used to mop the 'wetter' food up, remember we are eating with hands here. Lentils (my pet hate, Alison can eat mine), a curried vegetable or chicken if you have the non-veg (meat) option. The rest of the plate is what at home we would count as the accompaniments served up with papadums. Raita, pickles and chutneys and yes, we get papadums here too. A drink is served too and all of this was for the princely sum of sixty rupees, your money spent on food stretches so much further once you escape the tourist resorts of Goa!

The next day we were picked up from our hotel and set off towards Mysore. The bulk of the journey had been completed by the time we make our first stop of the day at the Daria Daulat Bagh. This is the first of the palaces that we are scheduled to visit, if Rajasthan is famed for its forts, Mysore has the same reputation for heritage structures and palaces! Daria Daulat Bagh translates as the 'Garden of the Sea of Wealth' and is in the city of Srirangapatna, ten miles or so shy of Mysore. In the scheme of what we have seen over the years it is plain, not helped by all the tarpaulins that are drawn to protect against damage from the sun. It is a squat teakwood building, rectangular in shape and built upon a raised platform. The open corridors along the four sides of the platform are all adorned with colourful but ancient frescoes in the style of Mysore paintings – at least now the huge numbers of tarpaulins make sense. The carved wooden pillars at the edges of the plinth are different, over the years it has predominantly been stonework that we have admired. Tipu Sultan, a man with the nickname of 'the Tiger of Mysore' built this palace in 1784 and ruled Mysore from here, but these days it is more famous for its gardens than anything else – and even they look dried and parched. It is safe to say that we were a little underwhelmed with our first stop...

Our next port of call, a very short drive away was more impressive, and the signage was also a lot more informative about who, why and when... The Gumbaz was built in Srirangapattana upon the orders of Tipu Sultan in 1782, and upon completion two years later it was to serve as the mausoleum for his mother and father. From what we can make out Tipu was the Capability Brown or Percy Thrower of his time, a great designer of landscapes and gardens. The mausoleum was surrounded by an impressive estate, with species of flowering trees and plants collected by Tipu Sultan himself from his travels around Persia, Turkey, Kabul and Mauritius. Within fifteen years of this monument being built Tipu himself would be buried here after his martyrdom in the Siege of Srirangapatna in 1799. The Gumbaz is Persian in design, standing on an elevated platform. The grand white dome is supported by thirty-six black granite pillars. Unusually the doors and windows have latticework cut from the same black granite, creating a simple but stunning contrast. If the outside is simplistic inside is a treat, the walls are painted with tiger stripes - after all he is known as the tiger of Mysore. Surrounding his resting place is a large rectangle garden with a path leading to the mausoleum. The three graves inside belong to Tipu Sultan, his father Hyder Ali and his mother Fakr-Un-Nisa, many of his 'lesser' relatives are buried outside the mausoleum in the perimeter of the garden. The original carved doors of the mausoleum have long been removed and are now displayed at the Victoria and Albert Museum, London.

Tipu Sultan met his end in the fourth Anglo – Mysore war. It was in the era of Napoleon; France and the soldiers of the British East India Company had been in conflict on and off for over thirty years by this point. Tipu Sultan as the ruler of the Kingdom of Mysore was a pioneer, an innovator; a new coinage system and calendar, implementation of a new land revenue system which initiated the growth of the Mysore silk industry. He was also responsible for the world's first war rocket, and two of these rockets captured by the British are displayed in the Royal Artillery Museum in London. His legacy remembers him as a fierce warrior king, one of the few Indian rulers to have ever defeated British armies.

Tipu died at the Siege of Seringapatam when the British won a decisive victory. The Mysore soldiers were vastly outnumbered, almost two to one, and surrounded on all sides. Defeat was inevitable. When the British armies broke through the city walls, French military advisers told Tipu Sultan to flee via secret passages and to fight the rest of the wars from other forts, but he refused. The expected happened, Tipu Sultan was killed at the Hoally Gateway and he was buried the following afternoon at the Gumaz, next to the grave of his father. The British allowed Tippu to be laid to rest with his family, respectful of his bravery and subsequent martyrdom - back home in Britain the death of Tipu Sultan was celebrated with declaration of a public holiday, authors, playwrights and painters creating works in celebration. And we had never even heard of him...

Our short onward journey to Mysore continues, and we are soon checked in at the Crystal Paark Inn. We have a few hours of daylight to explore Mysore for ourselves, finding the Mysore Palace should be easy enough but we also want to try the local sweet named after the city. Tomorrow morning our driver will pick us up and take us away from the city, to the outlying temples and the Nandi bull by the Chamundi Hills, but for the rest of today we are left to our own devices. Fortunately, it is an easy city to explore, or more a city that would be difficult to get lost in! There are no tight alleyways, or endless mazes – the streets here are wide, more like boulevards, tree-lined and with big traffic islands. When I say big, I mean big – one has a clock tower planted right in the middle, another bell-shaped canopy is the home to a large statue. With each roundabout being so distinctive it will be easy to navigate our way around, or at least the route from our hotel, to the local market and the Palace.

A giveaway clue that we are approaching the vicinity of the palace is the number of horses and carts, rows of attractive white carriages with red interiors are lined up behind equally white horses. We turn down the offer of a city tour and make our way along the approach road and through the arch. From the arch you get your first complete look at the Mysore Palace, also known as the Amba Vilas Palace – and describing it is going to be difficult... Let us start with the gardens, and the impressive bronze tigers - that is the easy bit; in total there are eight larger than life bronze tigers crouching on pedestals in the Mysore Palace complex. Six of them are in the grounds to the front of the palace, installed in pairs as if to guard the three pathways that approach the palace. The last pair are inside the building, which sadly we will not get to see as its under renovation. These big cats were sculpted in 1909 by Robert Williams Colton of the London Royal Academy of Arts... and he is also responsible for the chap on the roundabout, that marble statue mentioned earlier is one Jayachamarajendra Wodeyar, the last Maharaja of the Kingdom of Mysore (1940 to 1950).

The bronze tigers are impressive, who can resist not putting their wrist in the gaping mouth, sharp teeth looking like they can take your arm off at will. The lawn, or green scrub, makes up the bulk of the ground covering in the walled gardens, the wild flowers are ablaze with colour in the randomly placed beds, adding a vibrant natural look in the foreground of our photographs. Unfortunately for the gardener a lone cow is doing its best to undo his excellent work. Grand lampposts are in place, a single round light at the very top, with a further four round lights on a protruding 'X' about a foot lower down. More modern, high-powered lighting has been added below that, to light up the buildings and gardens rather than to be aesthetically pleasing.

Onto the Palace buildings... first my description and then the official architectural description. To my eye I would describe it as a cream-coloured building with multiple arches, mainly in pairs but sometimes in a group of three. Each corner block is made up of four towers and each tower is finished off with a red onion shaped dome. The official description says it was designed by Henry Irwin and is one of the finest achievements of Indo-Saracenic architecture, displaying examples of diverse themes that have been features of Indian architecture over the centuries. 'Muslim designs and Rajput style combined with Gothic elements and indigenous materials in an exuberant display of grandeur.' It goes on to talk about an intricately detailed elevation, delicately curved arches, bow-like canopies, magnificent bay windows and a range of styles of columns ranging from Byzantine to Hindu. The front of the palace façade has seven expansive arches, with two smaller ones flanking the central arch, each supported by tall pillars. High up, above the central arch is an impressive sculpture of Gajalakshmi - the Goddess of wealth with elephants.

Although much of the palace is closed for renovations, we can see the beauty of the ceilings through netting that hangs down over the arches. Our guess is that the mesh is there to prevent birds from flying inside and causing damage with their droppings. There is no doubt it is a beautiful building, covered in incredible frescoes but it is also relatively new – or at least compared to the other places that we have visited this morning and plan to see tomorrow. This version of the Mysore palace only dates back to 1912, the fourth reincarnation after the third was destroyed by fire in 1897. The history books suggest there has been a building on this site since the fourteenth century, more like a wooden fort in those early days. Tomorrow night we will get to see it fully illuminated, on every Sunday evening and national holidays ninety-seven thousand bulbs are switched on to light up the entire building and surrounding walls and arches - that promises to be a spectacular sight.

As the light begins to fade, we walk back towards the Crystal Paark Inn and see hundreds of green parrots, we have no idea where they have come from, but apparently they head to the nearby park each evening as the sun disappears. Amazed by the numbers of them we head back to our room to watch in comfort, our balcony looks right over their flight path. Tonight, having not explored far, we head to the hotel restaurant to eat and are pleased to find a buzzing busy atmosphere, rather than the dreaded more waiters than diners!

Sunday morning in Mysore and we get picked up bang on time, todays itinerary takes us out of town to the foot of the Chamundi Hills, and the similarly named Sri Chamundeshwari Temple. Of course, like every Indian temple there has to be a story behind it... legend says that the Goddess Durga slayed the demon king Mahishasura on the brow of this hill, and to the people of Karnataka they know it as Naada Devi - which means state Goddess. If slaying of demon kings is not enough how about an alternative, it is also said that the hair of Sati fell here. Sati, also known as Dakshayani, is the Hindu goddess of marital felicity and longevity.

It is another of those temples in the gopura desaign, multi-tiered and getting thinner as it reaches the top. Where some are covered heat to toes in carved images, often 'X-rated' this one is clean and crisp. A pastel yellow with just the two carved deities on each of the seven layers, and a further two on the tier just below the summit. The original shrine dates back to the twelfth century, and an indication of how high up the hill it is set, is that in 1659, a staircase of one thousand steps was built leading up to the nine hundred plus metre (three thousand foot) summit. Luckily for us these days there is a car park right outside, don't devotees get things easy these days? On our drive up we pass a huge image of Nandi (the bull mount of Shiva), that will be our stop off on the way back down.

In the shadows of the imposing temple is a market, initially we thought it was just flowers and garlands to lay as offerings in the temple being sold, but as we get closer it is any kind of tat; water pistols, plastic snakes, dolls clothes etc. The market is heaving though, of course there is the obligatory cow wandering around feasting on flower heads, before being shooed off by the stall holders. We have a wander around the outside first, enjoying the panoramic views from this elevated position, the city of Mysore nestling in the distance below. We take off our shoes and join the queue to enter the temple, there must be a festival going on, a band is playing and there are flowers everywhere you turn. Each pillar and door frame are bedecked in garlands and floral tributes and the sweet smell permeates through the whole place. As we approach one door we are almost carried through, such is the throng of people – Alison is certain her feet do not touch the floor until we reach the other side. When we get out our guide asks us if we see it? See what? In that heaving inner sanctum was a solid gold statue of the Goddess Durga.

Traffic is slow as we wind our way back down the hill, but our driver does find room to park close by the bull figure. This granite carving is believed to have been sculpted in the second century and at over fifteen feet high and twenty-four feet long it is an impressive sight. The relaxed looking bull is in a laid down pose, the detail is exquisite, braiding and tassels add some colour, cow bells hanging around its neck on a yellow chain. For some reason it has three white stripes, (adidas logo style), on its nose and further red and white piping, around its neck. Maybe it is a reference to the Tiger of Mysore; a cuddly, stuffed tiger has been placed on the wall, looking less than menacing.

Back in Mysore and we visit a final place of religion, the Roman Catholic Cathedral of St. Joseph and St. Philomena. Such a mouthful that locally it is referred to as plain old St. Joseph's. Constructed in 1936 using a Neo Gothic style its architecture was inspired by the Cologne Cathedral in Germany. While it is nothing out of the ordinary to visitors from Europe it is one of the tallest church buildings in the whole of Asia. Inside the church and you could be back at home – the wooden pews, alter and stained-glass windows, all remarkably familiar and traditional. One small detail sets it apart though - some of the female statues are depicted wearing Indian sarees.

As our driver takes us back to the hotel, he asks us if we would like to visit the Mysore Sand Sculpture Museum. Our plans for this afternoon are minimal, other than a wander around to hunt down some Mysore Pak, the sweet treat, we have nothing specific to do. The short journey takes us past our hotel until we reach a small car park outside one giant marquee. For a minimal entry fee, you get the opportunity to view over one hundred sculptures crafted from sand. It may well be aimed more at children but you cannot help but be impressed, there are scenes ranging from under the sea to the big five from the Serengeti. Tom and Jerry, Santa Claus, Egyptian Pharaohs, Julius Caeser and Red Indians – the list just goes on. Star of the show is a fifteen-foot statue of Lord Ganesha, followed closely by Lord Krishna and Arjuna on a horse-drawn chariot. The leaflet tells us that each of these depictions can last up to a year, despite being made from nothing more than sand, water and an insecticide spray to protect them from bugs. As we leave, we cannot help but smile; it was just easy viewing - pure fun!

For the rest of the afternoon we are on our own, and on a mission. We spotted a market on our walk yesterday – near to the palace and by the foot of the clocktower. As well as the local treat we are keen to try, we also need something a little more substantial to eat, a few pakoras or samosas would be perfect. We walk beyond the palace walls and the street sellers have their wares set out neatly on the floor, beautiful pyramids of oranges and apples. Further on and the fruits are immaculately displayed on old barrows, so colourful and with such care. Disappointingly for them, fruit is not on our agenda, we want something far unhealthier than that! It is not too long before we have arranged our two courses, the smoke from the frying fat and the sight of a queue of people as they wait for freshly cooked samosas attracts our attention. With them wrapped up in newspaper we source the desert.

Mysore Pak is fit for a King, and so it should be – it was first made on the orders of the Maharaja of Mysore, Krishna Raja Wadiyar IV. Madappa, his chef, began experimenting, wanting to present the King with something new and unusual. The Maharaja loved the sweet so much that he asked Madappa what it was called, he blurted out the first thing that came to mind, - 'Mysore Pak'. Pak, refers to the sticky sugar syrup achieved by simmering sugar with an equal amount of water; the syrup is flavoured with a spice mix, a skilled art mastered by few chefs who keep their exact methods secret. If Krishna Raja Wadiyar IV, the Maharaja of Mysore who it was created for needed a dentist he could afford one... At the time of his death in 1940, he was one of the world's wealthiest men, with a personal fortune estimated to be worth four-hundred million US dollars (the equivalent of a little over eight billion in 2022).

The original sweet made with that original recipe is still available at the famous Guru Sweets stores in Devaraja Market, ran by the great-grandsons of Madappa. Our verdict: Texture wise it is somewhere between fudge, and a buttery dense cookie. If you have ever eaten jaggery it is not dissimilar to that - tooth-rottingly sweet, but so delicious and very moreish, to be avoided if you are watching your weight!

As well as enjoying the local sugar-laden sweets we accidentally end up going to see Mysore incense sticks being prepared, not on a mass scale, but more home production. We were just browsing them on a local store when the stallholder's son asked if we would like to see them being made? Earlier I said that Mysore is a city you could not get lost in, I was wrong – from the market we are led through a warren of streets and passageways to the base of a stairwell for some flats... These steps were occupied by local ladies rolling the sticks in a gungy mix that smelt far better than it looked. Our impromptu guide who spoke a little English explained how they were then taken up the stairs to dry out on the rooftops. We ended up buying five or six packs, these had a story to tell rather than those picked from the shelves of a random souvenir shop. Despite our purchase we were still abandoned by the young salesman, and left to find our own way back to the market...

In India, these sticks, or agarbathi as they call them, have been awarded the Geographical Indication tag by the government. A bit like our Melton Mowbray pork pies, they must be produced in the Mysore region to bear that moniker. The sticks made in Mysore are all from locally grown ingredients that are only found in Karnataka, and whilst the world's biggest producer of them is based here so are hundreds of individual households, making them by hand. It is a simple procedure; a blend of herbs, flowers, oils, barks, roots and charcoal are finely ground into a smooth paste and then rolled on to the sandalwood stick until it is fully coated. We suspect that the world's biggest producer has something more technical to bake it dry than relying on the sun?

With our tick list successfully completed all that was left was tonight's visit to Mysore Palace, to witness it in all its illuminated glory, could it live up to our expectations? We arrive in good time, its busy but not packed and as daylight fades the lamps in the grounds come on, lighting up both the palace and walk ways. With one eye on our watches, we wait for 7 p.m., light up time; with a blink of an eye the whole palace, gateways and walls are bathed by the specially manufactured bulbs. It is a breath-taking sight, we thought it might be a gradual process – but no, one switch and they are all on. The forty-five minutes that they are on for provides ample time for another, and for us a final wander around the grounds, taking photographs from all angles, trying different settings on the camera to get a perfect shot. It has been well worth the visit, and for anyone considering an excursion to Mysore be sure to arrange it with the Sunday evening illuminations in mind. It is back to eat at the Crystal Paark Inn, one of the best hotel restaurants we have had, in fact from our review we liked everything about our stay there...

Hotel with a buzzing restaurant

Review of Hotel Crystal Paark Inn

Lovely hotel, very central & handy for Mysore Palace. Room was comfortable, shower fantastic. Normally we avoid hotel restaurants as they can often be lacking in atmosphere - not here. the food was great, reasonably priced & the restaurant had plenty of guests / customers in.

It also has a 'pub' style bar, again a few customers in but we found it very smoky (guess years of No Smoking in public places in England meant it was a shock of how things used to be).

Would definitely return if visiting Mysore again.

Room tip: Park views, don't give much of a park view but you do see 100's of parrots in the trees at the side early evening as it gets dark.

Next day its travel all the way, Mysore to Bangalore by car and then an onward flight back to Goa before we are picked up from the airport and ferried back to Calangute. Everything runs smooth, traffic was busy around Bangalore, but nothing like as hectic as when we had arrived there a few days ago. We departed from Bangalore on time and our driver was in Goa waiting for us. All was running like clockwork until we were driving over one of the big bridges, suddenly the sound of the road changed completely – strange noises, and not of the good type. Our driver has no option but to continue driving until he was off the bridge, pulling over at the first opportunity once we had crossed. The issue did not take a qualified mechanic for the diagnosis, a back tyre as flat as a pancake – or chapati, considering where we are. How the situation ends we do not really know, our driver started flagging other cars down – surely some of them must be heading to Calangute? Within a matter of minutes, we have a lift back secured - our journey continues. Our good Samaritan speaks minimal English, but we are assured by our driver that he will drop us off home; we were naturally a little apprehensive, we do not know this young guy from Adam – in a country of a billion plus people we have got in a car with a stranger, something we would never do at home! Thankfully, after all our times over the years back and forth to the airport we recognise the route, or are at least familiar with certain landmarks, and before long we are home, dropped right on the doorstep of the Casa Aleixo.

What is left of our time in Goa is the usual; pool or beach, followed by early evening samosas with either a beer or a cup of tea. If we have returned to the balcony to eat then we get the added bonus of a sheet of newspaper to read, there is something that tickles us about the words they use to describe things. One story we remember was about someone being killed in a bus queue when a scooter ploughed into the waiting passengers, the headline described it as a 'traffic mishap.' We count a mishap as breaking a plate or spilling your coffee – they use flippant descriptions however tragic the situation or incident. Our evenings continue in the same manner, a meal out and then the plastic chairs of Madhu's, hopefully on the front row for a prime seat of tonight's entertainment passing before our eyes.

In no time our two weeks are over, departing Dabolim is our smoothest yet. With the Thomas Cook or Thomson flight you have three hundred or so passengers turning up on mass, sometimes the queue to get your case scanned and stickered runs outside the doors! Qatar Airways had their own scanners, the check in desks were fully staffed with no one waiting - this was like Dabolim airport heaven. Of course, it is the same immigration control you must pass through, but with no chartered flights heading out even that is a doddle. Our flight out was barely half full, and once the plane was airborne and the seatbelts sign off, we moved and enjoyed a whole centre row each.

Most years when we arrive home, one of our first priorities is to book next year's holiday – this time we didn't, perhaps we had a sixth-sense?

January to March 2016 — Goa and Varanasi

This year a different route to Goa altogether... following redundancy last year we had been enjoying some time travelling. We left England over two months earlier, Bangkok and onto Chiang Mai before travelling through Cambodia and the entire length of Vietnam before heading back to Bangkok...

We left Bangkok for Goa, not on the most direct of flights but the cheapest, via Kuala Lumpur. Anyone who knows their geography will realise the first leg to KL is in the wrong direction! It was all down to the cost; our time was plentiful so the quickest route was not as important. Our Air Asia departure is delayed due to military flyovers going on, in celebration of Thailand's Children Day. Kuala Lumpur airport is much of a blur, having the first part of our flight delayed means that it is a whistle-stop visit, we follow the transit passenger signs and are soon waiting to board our second flight of the day. This one is a squashed, cramped experience, for some reason Indian passengers always have crazy amounts of hand luggage with them, by the time we board the overhead lockers are full so our hand luggage is wedged under the seats in front.

Welcome to India and the queues for immigration control. Our pen does not write on their forms, yet the books we purchased in Bangkok are covered in bits of scribble – it is not the pen that is faulty! We do manage to borrow a pen from someone else but that is almost as bad, we finally manage to scrawl our details in a very scruffy fashion onto the form. Everyone is having the same issue, dodgy paper... think Izal toilet paper from your schooldays! Filling in the form was the trickiest part; the bags were already circling on the carousel by the time we got through and our driver was there holding up a name card as we exit the airport building. It is a steady drive to Calangute, North Goa, which will be our home for a little over two months. As we approach the town itself there are signs of life, its approaching midnight by this point so while the restaurants have closed some of the bars are still open.

Valerie, who we have arranged the apartment through has given the keys to our driver, so he is able to lead us straight to the door and let us in. We are located just off the main road, on the ground floor of a small apartment block; exploring inside we are impressed, a spacious living room, good sized bedroom with air-conditioning, kitchen (complete with a washing machine) and a bathroom. We get into bed, and then have to search for an extra sheet

– the air conditioning had been on when we arrived, it obviously works well as the room is a bit on the cool side.

We sleep well, and although the main road is only fifty metres or so away, we cannot hear anything at all, it is a chicken that has brought are sleep to an end. We make ourselves a coffee and figure out the much-needed washing machine, it is obviously brand new as it still has all the labels on, but it loads from the top. We have no powder or anything but run through a wash of essentials regardless, in another change from our normal visits we have arrived here with a case of dirty clothes. Alison does like a list, so is in her element creating a first shop. In the kitchen we also have a fridge with a small freezer compartment at the top, a two-ring gas stove and a kettle, so cooking for ourselves is now an option. Cleaning products also need to be on our first shop, washing up liquid, wash powder, a small scrubbing brush etc. Overall, we are more than satisfied with what we have got.

We go out onto the main road and realise exactly where we are, a perfect location for us as our favourite bar, Madhu's, is just a hundred metres or so to the right. Walking down the road the other way, to the left is the Calangute roundabout, we pass the Lambada Hotel where we have stayed before and recognise a lot of the restaurants that we have eaten in, it is like coming home! After a failed shopping mission, we head back along the Baga road back towards our apartment, which is situated in a block standing behind the Union Bank of India. Valerie has her travel agency / money exchange in a small office that is part of that block, so we are practically neighbours.

We head into Madhu's where we are greeted enthusiastically by the guys who run it, we have been regulars in here for a good number of years and just love the simplicity of the place. Another tradition of that first meal at Mirabai's is observed, Chilli Chicken. Alison goes for the vindaloo and we share the two dishes between us, a definite thumbs up but lacking a bit of the fiery heat that we had hoped for! On our way back to our apartment we are intercepted by an elderly couple, they had seen us leaving our room this morning and it turns out that they are Valerie's Mum and Dad, Esme and Michael. We introduce ourselves; Michael is a huge cricket fan and Esme loves cooking – over the next few weeks we get to sample a few of her dishes!

Our afternoon is spent sorting through our luggage, we finally have a wardrobe to hang things up in, the remainder of the dirty washing is left in the bags awaiting washing powder. We bring in the sweeping brush from the veranda and run that around the place, the mopping will also have to wait until we have cleaning products. Flicking through TV channels we are delighted to see that we have Star Sports, so we will be able to catch up on the football. Having watched the early kick-off we get ready to go out, only to find out that we have minimal hot water, well minimal water. We manage a quick wash before heading to Krishna's for our tea, two curry meals in one day – we will end up huge if we keep this up!

We pop back to Madhu's and are pleased to see that a local character, Chef, is sat in his usual seat, there are also a lot of other faces we recognise from previous years – we are not the only creatures of habit! Service has improved, ice is readily available whereas other years tracking down the ice bucket used to be a case for Inspector Morse. We get chatting to Chef, everyone refers to him as that - he is a fantastic cook and makes pies for some of the local restaurants and customers of Madhu's. He also does a range of cookies that have his special magical ingredient... It turns out that he has had an eventful year, and not in a good way, not only had he the misfortune to fall and broke his hip but he had also been arrested for possession of one of the key elements to his cookies! There is never a dull moment when the Chef is around...

There is still no water when we turn the taps on first thing. At least we have some bottled water so can still make coffee. A knock on the door and the whirlwind that is Valerie comes in, full of hugs and welcomes. She is looking very well, happy that we like the apartment and pleased to see us, as we are her. It is a flying visit as she has her shop to open, we say that we will pop in a little later to catch up with her husband Savio and their daughter Sovann too.

A trip to the nearby supermarket fulfils half of our shopping list, a trip to one of the bigger stores will be needed too. Heading off into town we soon track down the missing items in the Bombay Bazaar; on our return home we can now sweep and mop the floor, water has been restored! Another load of washing done and hung out before we head down to the beach, but not before stopping at the Infantaria for lunch. Infantaria, is part bakery, part restaurant – but serves fantastic food and snacks. We opt for a mix of quiches, samosas and egg chops (like scotch eggs, but spicier).

Our afternoon is spent on the beach, we walk down the steps, turning left until we reach the Rovers Return beach shack. The sun is not too hot, or its more the case that the breeze is keeping us cool. We have a drink and people watch, there is always beach sellers trying to make a living but also with one eye out for the local plod who will confiscate all their goods given half a chance. There is not much you cannot buy; speakers, fruit, massage, shawls, clothing, drums, maps, watches – if it can be carried then it can be sold on the beach. We return home, quickly visiting Valerie on the way back, we have some money to collect from her. Savio and Sovann are both looking well and we cannot believe how Sovann has grown since we last see her; unfortunately, we have no English chocolate for her on this occasion!

Food wise we try somewhere new tonight, Chick and Fish on the main road, chosen as much because it looked busy. The chicken cafreal and chicken chilli fry were both tasty and spice laden. We will certainly eat here again. Back in Madhu's we have a prime slot, the tables right at the front mean that you can then rest your feet on the wall! It is not long before a couple we have met the other year arrive, Mike and Sylvia are both looking well. We have a quick chat but they are out with another couple tonight – we will get a proper catch up another night...

The first Honey Bee hangover, our heads are buzzing this morning! Nothing that cannot be worked through, an additional cup of coffee sees it off before another trip to the supermarket in Calangute. Tea, sugar, rice and some spice mixes; we are getting set for cooking our own meals some evenings. It is our first ever visit to the 'chicken shop,' or Royals as its nameboard says, it sells chickens and not much else, legs, mince, breasts, whole... if its chicken Royals will have it. They sell eggs too. Returning through the market and we pick up some bananas, we are laden down by now, so the vegetables that we need will have to wait until tomorrow.

The afternoon is again spent on the beach, the sea is rough and Alison is hanging onto her bottoms as she comes back up after being completely knocked off her feet by a wave! The waves are great fun but tiring, it really is a job to keep your footing as they crash over you. Walking back home we pick up some samosas and batatawadas from the guy who sets up daily outside the Red Lion Pub at around 4 p.m., wrapped up in newspaper they will keep warm to eat with a nice cup of tea. It turns out that what we thought was sugar isn't, once we have Wi-Fi Google translate tells us that it is a vitamin supplement.

On the topic of Wi-Fi; whilst it is everywhere and easily accessible in Cambodia and Vietnam it is not so easy to come by, or the reliability as good, here in Goa. It seems strange as everyone automatically thinks of India as the world leader for out-sourced call centres, perhaps we need to buy ourselves a SIM card for the data package? For this evening though we need to find a connection - we have a drink in the Cricketers, but sadly their Wi-Fi is no good. Our next try is more successful, Mirabai's for a meal, the prawn Vindaloo is divine, and even more so when the owner of the restaurant recommends adding a few chopped onions and lime juice, beautiful! The Wi-

Fi connection in here is also good, so we can catch up with emails, check in on home etc. A Kingfisher beer or two in Madhu's round off this evening, Chef is sat in there and he has brought us his price list – a good old pie will be on our dinner plates before too long...

We are both as fit as fiddles this morning, the early night has done us some good. As we venture out Valerie is putting her boards out, advertising her excursions and currency exchange rates. We tell her about our shopping expedition yesterday and she 'tells' us that she will give us a cooking lesson, half past twelve tomorrow – and that if we pop back in later, she will have a list of ingredients that we will need. We take the opportunity to ask if the apartment owner could get us a toaster, our breakfast options are a bit limited!

Over the years I have bought leather slip on sandals from the same guy who sells them on Beach Road, we spotted him on our way back from the sea front yesterday. They are some of the comfiest that I have ever had and the quality is exceptionally good too, today I am hopeful of buying a new pair. He remembers us, and he has the usual style that I go for, a straightforward slip on, nothing between the toes as I find that uncomfortable. That is me easily sorted, price negotiated and bought. Alison sees some that she likes but just not in her size – hers will have to be especially made and be ready for collection in a few days!

As we go down the lane by Valerie's shop, she comes out brandishing not only a shopping list but also a toaster for us, unfortunately it has a crack; so close to getting a cooked breakfast! Valerie advises us that the horn we hear each night around six thirty is the bread man making his deliveries, and if you pop out to him you can buy fresh pav buns, that sounds like a plan. With that in mind we pop to the little supermarket nearby and buy a bag of eggs, no such thing as cartons here, just a little see-through plastic bag. With cooking ourselves tomorrow we don't order any pies from Chef, instead we opt for his home-made pate, another breakfast option, once we have that toaster! A few beers ensue and a small bottle of the Honey Bee brandy...

Breakfast, wow! Fried eggs in buttery pav buns and a splash of tomato sauce, simplistic but heavenly. The yolks are bright orange, free range is standard here and the tomato sauce has subtle spicing to it rather than our version. We have plenty of chicken from our shopping the other day, the rest of the list means a trip to the market, onions, tomatoes and potatoes. We smile as the lady at the market put all three items on the scales together, rather than individually like you would at home. Total price is forty rupees, so with the current exchange rate that is forty pence.

Bang on time and Valerie arrives at our apartment, not empty-handed either – a toaster! Our cookery lesson is not only entertaining but also a great learning curve; we both cook at home but there is an enormous difference between following a recipe and being shown by a particularly good cook of exactly how to treat the spices to get the best flavour. Today's lesson will cover a vegetable pilau rice, chicken Vindaloo and a riata dip, Valerie makes everything look so easy, from the chopping and dicing all the way through to the cooking, and with what we would count as limited equipment. The smells are making us hungry, cannot wait to eat that this evening!

After cleaning everything up afterwards, washing up etc, we pop out for a couple of beers – it got ridiculously hot in that kitchen! Sitting by the wall with our feet up, drinking ice-cold Kingfisher, does life get much better this? The road in front of us is getting busier, during the week its mostly scooters and taxis, today there are plenty of big four by four cars that are negotiating their way past all the obstacles, think cows, dogs, tourists... Goa is extremely popular with domestic tourists at weekends and on public holidays; it is so different to any other Indian state, far more relaxed and liberal than the rest of the country – they all flock here to let their hair down and party! The festival of Makara Sankranti celebrates the Hindu sun god Surya, meaning a public holiday, and it seems that many have booked extra days off to take full advantage of it

It is the time of day where we switch the television on; while reheating the feast that 'we' cooked this afternoon we watch MasterChef Asia, the last few days have had us hooked, hopefully something we can learn from watching that too. Our meal is delicious, on a par with restaurant food, we would love to be able to cook that well ourselves. The vegetable pilau is more than just a rice accompaniment, it is a great tasting dish, and there will be some of that left over for tomorrow. By the time we leave for home we will be the size of a house, we need to remember that this is not just a two week stay, we need to pace ourselves...

Next morning and its housework, we have almost forgotten what that is like having spent two months living in hotels, hostels and guest houses. We are not untidy by any means, pots are always washed and dried, but it is the sand – it gets everywhere! A thorough sweep up and mop should stop us trailing it into our bed, plus I give the bathroom a once over too. The bathroom is more a wet room, so with a slight turn of the shower head you could wash while sitting on the toilet! A lip of a centimetre is all that separates the toilet and the basin from the shower section, so the water bounces off your body and then drains back, leaving the sand behind. Each day we swill the sand away but it is a constant battle. With our jobs done we head down to the beach, at the foot of the Calangute steps the beach is heaving with Indian visitors. They are having a fun time – the vendors hiring out the jet-skis and parasailing experiences must be raking it in. What makes us smile is that the Indian ladies venture in the sea wearing their saris, very few Indian men have proper swimming gear either, stripping down to their pants is classed as beach-ready!

I guess living in the UK most of us grow up experiencing days on the beach through our childhood? For many Indians a beach is a new experience, and fair play to them, the inner child comes out; they play the games we all did growing up, burying each other in the sand seems to be the favourite! We have a chilled afternoon, a dish of spiced chips at the Rovers Return and a couple of lime sodas before heading back up beach road towards home. No sign of the shoe seller today, and we are too early for the samosa guy so a bag of 'Masala Munch' crisps for an afternoon snack today – along with what remains of the vegetable pilau!

Tonight's meal is at another one of our favourite restaurants when we are in Goa, though we normally only visit the once, on the last evening before a flight home. The Tibetan Kitchen does a fantastic beef steak, with crushed potatoes and a delicious side salad; it tasted every bit as good as before but a little pricier than we recalled, never mind it is an attractive setting for a bit of a treat. Like most evenings we finish off in Madhu's, Chef has brought us a tub of the pate we had ordered – so after a couple of beers we go home, fire up the toaster and share a sample slice between us...

On Saturday there is a local market, which we had somehow never discovered before - you can buy almost anything. It is the fruit and vegetables that we have gone for but if we wanted padlocks, shoelaces, jeans or towels we would have been successful too. The prices are incredibly low, even for our white faces! We buy some more spices, bananas and strawberries, the rest of the vegetables we will pick up from the covered market, purely because it is closer to home and less of a distance to carry.

Our afternoon is spent cooking, another chicken vindaloo, Bombay spuds (more my recipe from at home), Alison creates a riata as a dip and a vegetable pilau rice, but the texture is not as good as the Valerie assisted attempt though. We have done bigger portions this time, with plenty of live football on we can eat at home, save costs and enjoy the match while we eat. There is enough food here for both Saturday and Sunday. With our earlier cooking reheated and dished up we get sat down and watch the first game. The food is an enormous success, and whilst the vegetable rice does not have the fluffy texture it is still very eatable! Our plans to watch the second game are interrupted by a lack of cable signal, so it is an early night with a book.

Breakfast has turned into a daily fried egg in a pav bun (more on the pav bun in a little while). The toaster is getting plenty of use too, and Chef's pate is a regular treat! Alison gets her new hand-made shoes collected from the guy on Beach Road, they fit perfectly. Wi-Fi, or at least access continues to be a pain at most places, we have a couple of 'go to' places so that we are still managing to stay connected with everyone back home. We've both had haircuts, a tiny shop on the Baga road, about eye-level to the road once you have gone down the steps, I go first and he does an excellent job for the one hundred rupees. Alison is that impressed that the following day she pays the same for a trim herself, she did have a couple of beers beforehand to steady her nerves though!

Other discoveries include our new favourite dish, Hyderabad biriyani; we often order this instead of a rice dish and then we go for a naan instead. Paneer, absolutely love it – just not something we had considered in the past. On the days when we visit the food market, we have taken to having lunch at the Café Anan, a proper locals place with prices to match, we have Valerie to thank for that tip as we would never have considered it otherwise. We have two of each; samosas, batatawadas, egg chops, cups of chai and cake, all for ninety-four rupees, less than one English pound!

A Sunday dinner at the Rovers Return provides a taste of home, it is so popular that you must book a time slot. It did initially seem strange sitting on the beach eating a full roast dinner but it compared well to pub lunches that we have had at home. If we were to be overly fussy, the mash potato was 'sloppier' than we like, but otherwise it was brilliant. Cooking for ourselves we have been making pav bhaji, pav being the bun and bhaji being nothing like an onion bhaji! The packet mix of that name is added to tomatoes, onions, grated carrots, peas, potatoes, so in English terms the vegetables are all cooked together and then mashed, so a spicy mashed potato fusion served in a warm bun... In addition to our home cooking, we sometimes get food parcels from Valerie's Mum, no wonder our clothes are shrinking...

Prawns... they are massive compared to what we get at home! Valerie orders them and then we pay her for them, like most things in Goa a white face pays far more than a local. We are given a quick lesson in preparing them and some masala (blend of spices) to cook them in, really, really tasty – there not something we eat much of at home as there so expensive, it is a special treat, it feels like we are spoiling ourselves!

The Pav buns... it turns out the breadman has been ripping us off! By chance we happen to be in Valeries shop when the breadman passes by, Valerie orders from him and gets seven pav buns for her twenty rupees; he has been charging us ten rupees each – you should get three for that! We are not sure what Valerie said to him, but the next night he was very sheepish, and we are charged correctly from that day on.

It is while sitting in Madhu's one afternoon that we can now say beyond all doubt, Indian women work far harder than their male counterparts... Roadworks are going on right outside, no mechanical equipment, no safety shoes either, in fact no shoes at all - just pickaxes and shovels. The man has taken charge of leaning on the shovel while the woman is left to wield the pickaxe, she is striking blow after blow while he just shovels occasionally, just to keep it clear for her! We had noticed on another night that women do all the carrying, if their hands are full some will balance stuff on their heads - while the bloke walks behind emptyhanded...

Most evenings we end up in Madhu's, exceeding our alcohol units each week. I have moved onto the Old Monk rum while Alison sticks to the Honey Bee, a can of coke suits us both as the mixer. We catch up with Mike and Sylvia and their friends, Ken and Mo. With no live music and with tables limited, we often share with others, you get to meet some interesting people and the strangest of conversations. The drinks flow, spirits are bought by the bottle, albeit 180ml sized ones. Your bill is tallied up at the end, calculated from your empties; by the end of the night your table is full of empty cans, maybe a couple of empty beer bottles and occasionally two empty spirit bottles each. We never had a bill that cost more than six pounds, you cannot get a drink each for that at home in many places! Unsurprisingly there has been the odd hangover...

February starts badly, SpiceJet have changed our flight schedule for Varanasi, their change means that we now arrive in Delhi late in the afternoon but do not depart for Varanasi until the next morning – nightmare! Valerie comes to our rescue, no doubt it helps that she is a booking agent, but by the end of the day we have better flights than our original booking! Rather than flying via Delhi we now transit through Hyderabad, the waiting around time is good too, comfortable rather than tight!

G and M Jewellers has a fantastic reputation, so going on that we walk out towards Baga and Alison takes her rings for a combination of repair, replate and polish; one for each. The price seems very reasonable at just under ten pounds for all that work. We are slightly worried at leaving that amount of value with him, I guess back at home a jewellers would have insurance in place in case of loss or damage? Fingers crossed... A remarkably close encounter with a cow got our hearts racing on the way home! Walking side by side this cow come charging around the corner at full speed and passes right between us; this bovine was far nimbler than we thought possible, for that split second it seemed like it had to hit us!

Walking past the Casa Aleixo, a place where we have stayed at once before, we meet Mr. Wilfred whose family home it is. Built in a traditional Portuguese style it is our favourite place to stay when in Goa by far, it sits back nicely from the road, has a small swimming pool and Mr. Wilfred is an interesting guy. They are a lovely couple but also very selective of who gets to stay in their home, luckily, he likes us! He says to pop in at some point before we leave, and we will take him up on that.

The jewellers did an amazing job, what were we worrying about? They really do look like new, the one that was repaired now looks in pristine condition. He does try upselling as we collect them, Alison's eyes light up but we do leave with nothing... As the jeweller shows, most people can be trusted, not all though; every two or three weeks I send a postcard home to Mum and Dad, on the third occasion the cashier at the Post Office tries to hugely overcharge us for a stamp – it was like 'pavgate' all over again!

Our days on the beach are still enjoyable, in the past our attention span means that within an hour or two we are bored. Second hand bookshops have been the key to our beach success, a constant supply of reading material means that we are quite content in the sunbeds. Some days we spend a lot of time in the sea, others it is just too rough; I am ok with drawstring trunks, Alison is in danger of indecency charges – crashing waves have no respect for dignity, top half or bottom... The shacks provide sunbeds free of charge, they make their living from guests eating and drinking there – fair enough. We opt for food at midday, a light snack to keep us going, but sometimes a breakfast too. They make fantastic milkshakes, sell beer obviously and plenty of water to rehydrate, we are spending six hours there some days, putting a proper shift in!

Alison is so impressed with her hand-made shoes that she orders a second pair, for leather sandals you just cannot go wrong, they wear well and are as comfortable as slippers. Not to be left out I treat myself to a new sunhat, the one from Vietnam is so faded and stained by sweat. Cooking wise we are improving, for the first time ever I have cooked a decent biriyani, that has always been my Achilles heel, I am over the moon with that. Valerie drops in various food bits, not always Indian either, cheese filled potato croquets on one occasion. Esme, Valeries mum, sends us fish dishes around; she obviously doesn't think we are starving because she happily points out that we are packing the weight on! Add into the mix occasional pies from the Chef, and pate too, we are living very well.

We discover different routes into town, rather than going via the main road and up to the roundabout every time we can continue along the track behind our apartment. Proper road soon gives out to a sandy, dusty track, concrete buildings turn into tarpaulin and tin-roofed living quarters, to be honest it takes us a little by surprise, we have seen such builds in other parts of India but not in Goa since our first stay at the Aldeio Bello. Chana, as in a chana masala means chickpea – I did go hungry that day, Alison had to eat the whole lot as I cannot stand them! Café Anan has no descriptions by the dishes, just the local name – so the only way to find out is by ordering one, on the plus side the cake we had also ordered was now all mine...

A tea bag crisis takes some resolving, for some reason we cannot find any anywhere! Loose tea is on sale by the bucket load, and its two full days before we track the 'bagged' variety down. It is while on the great tea bag hunt that we see our first scooter prang, for this trip I had got an International Driving Permit, planning to hire a moped so we could explore further. Once we arrived in Goa and remember the chaos on the roads, we promptly dismiss that idea, it is just not the right place for someone with no experience.

Evenings are more of the same; if we have not cooked ourselves, we are alternating between a handful of restaurants - Carvalho's, Chick and Fish, Krishna, Mirabai's and the Kindman. The Kindman is known for its pork chops and more English style food, but we love it for its chicken vindaloo, they do not hold back on the heat! It was Ken and Mo who tipped us off about this place, it is one of their regular haunts. If you want a hot, hot curry have a word with Peter, the guy who takes your orders – ask for it 'Ken hot' and you will have your eyes watering and be sniffing while you eat! Most evenings we sit and chat with Mike and Sylvia in Madhu's, they are always good company and share the same sense of humour. Sylvia even convinces us that Feni, the local alcohol brew is not as bad as we remember, served long with lemonade it is rather nice...

Valerie, Savio and Sovann take us out for a meal too, a restaurant called Fortunes that is out of town. We all squeeze into Savios car and make the short journey away from the coast (we are not sure where, but certain we travel inland!). The food is outstanding, the chicken cafreal is one we have never tried before, but from now on is added to our list of regular choices. The coated fried mussels were something else that we would never order either, they know what dishes are good and it is an opportunity for us to try new foods, knowing it will not be wasted if we don't like it.

On the food front, chai kulfi (tea flavoured ice-cream). Something else we discovered on the walk back from the beach; before if we had an ice-cream we had gone with the 'Qwality Walls' bike sellers, the same Walls brand from back home. The kulfi sellers are more independents, no fancy trolley bikes, just a huge tub mounted on the back and a scoop, but so creamy and tasty. An evening meal discovery is the Rock Café, or more precisely, their steaks. Nothing fancy, a chunk of steak and chips; as much as we both love curry there is a breaking point where you fancy something more familiar!

We have a catch up with Wilfred at the Casa Aleixo, he is looking very well. He invites us in for drinks on the terrace with a group of ladies that he has staying there, from what we gather they are old friends, some from Mumbai and others from Delhi but they meet up in Goa occasionally. They are all very chatty and interesting company; Wilfred is full of it in host mode and keeps the beers flowing. After an hour or so we make our excuses, and leave him in the company of the ladies...

Valerie and Savio invite us for a meal at their home, along with another English couple who they are good friends with. Savio kindly picks us up and takes us to their apartment in Para Towers, from what we see it looks a very modern development and their place is lovely, very stylish. Some of their church families are also there and it is a great evening of excellent food and interesting conversation. We are not religious in any way, and fortunately the evening was not too heavy or didn't get uncomfortable for us. Whilst they sang praise the English contingent sat it out on the balcony, but a great night and good to share different opinions and experiences.

Varanasi. One of the oldest cities in the world and by this evening we will be there. For anyone who is fascinated by India then they will already know a lot about this holy place, we have seen programme after programme on it, but now we are going to get to experience it for ourselves. As usual we check about a dozen times that we have our passports and tickets that Valerie has printed off for us. Collected on time and dropped off at Goa airport within the same hour, the day has started smoothly and continues that way, no flight delay. There is no luggage for us to check in so we are soon through to the departure lounge, and before we know it, we are on the short walk to our awaiting plane...

Today we are to board a Bombardier Q400 – and it has no jets just a propeller! It seems so small; boarding is at the rear where the stairs are part of the plane once it has been folded back up, and at just seventy-eight seats, two either side of the aisle it seems tiny. I must admit I was nervous, but once in the air it was a smooth journey – landing was a bit rougher but overall enjoyed the experience. The changeover in Hyderabad runs on time and we are soon boarding onto a more standard plane. Just like the first flight we are the only white faces onboard, lots of children mean it is not the quietest or most relaxing flight! To complete the experience sprinkle in a bout of turbulence that delayed the meal service, we were well ready to get off by the time we arrived in Varanasi. With no luggage to collect or passport control with it being a domestic flight we are soon heading towards the exit.

A driver arranged by the Baba Guesthouse is already waiting for us as we leave the airport building, but before we can set off, he must search for the driver of a car who has blocked him in! It only delays our journey for a few minutes before we set off with Bangla music playing on the car stereo. He tells us his name is Babaloo but we do not think he knows many words of English. As we approach the city it is crazy, yes, we have hit rush hour; cars, cows, motorbikes, cycles – you name it, everything is jockeying for position and not prepared to give an inch! It takes an hour to crawl through the last couple of miles before he pulls over and phones the Guesthouse for someone to collect us.

It takes five minutes for him to get here, we climb out and he tells us to follow him... We are led down a warren of small alleys, dodging bikes, cow dung and cows; these alleys are tight, there is no way to give them a wide berth, you are brushing up each other. For the first time on our travels the question 'what have we done?' goes through our mind, this place is daunting – how will we ever find our way around these mazes on our own? After what seemed like an age, we reach the Baba Guesthouse and are given a welcome cup of chai while we get checked in, the sweetness of the chai must be good for our shock. Our room is compact but clean, the bathroom is nice. We ask about food but none is available; we do not fancy venturing out; its dark by now and we are not convinced we would find our way back, so we finish the rest of our biscuits. Tonight, is an exceedingly early bed time, we get cosy under our furry blanket, hoping against hope that we can evade the mosquitoes...

A new morning and with a more positive mindset, we had both slept well and somehow have not been eaten alive! It is still quite early, before eight anyway, and we have no breakfast option here at the Baba Guesthouse, so off we go. The first corner we turn and there is a restaurant, also called Baba, how handy is that - if only we had known last night! We order parathas, curd and chai, it will at least start us off for the day. As we sit and eat our breakfast a cow wanders by, pauses and looks in at us, as if it were considering a meal itself. We settle our bill and say 'Ghats?,' they seem to understand and point which way we want to be – back past our guesthouse...

First turn after our guesthouse and we get our first glimpse of the Ganges and within a minute, after stepping over several sleeping dogs, we are on Munshi Ghat. The word ghat means a series of steps leading down to water, Varanasi is made up of eighty-eight of them; many of them form one long continuous promenade, so you can walk a good distance and take in daily life on the Ganges. This is the Holiest of all places for Hindus, to die and have your funeral here is their life's wish. They believe that the Ganges River is the most holy of rivers and for their ashes to be immersed here is the ultimate salvation. We are not walking for long at all before we reach one of the burning ghats, Harishchandra; in the distance, closer to the river is a shrouded body on a bed of wood, waiting to be set alight. It is too early in the morning to be taking any of that in so we continue our walk.

Further along we arrive at a bathing ghat; a mix of men, women and children are all going through their morning rituals. On a wall by the steps a mirror is propped up as ladies do their hair, on the steps barbers are giving haircuts and shaves to their customers, no disposable razors, cut throat ones rinsed in a bucket of water. It feels quite intrusive just being here, it is hard to imagine going through your daily hygiene routine in full view of the passing world. Next ghat along, and more bathers – only this time it is a herd of buffalo. Their herder is in the river with them and he is giving them a good brushing, and they look like they are really enjoying it! Its barely gone 9:30 a.m. and our minds are already blown; yes, we have seen it on the TV but to witness it with your own eyes is something else. It is incredible how in such a short distance there are bodies being burnt, buffalo's bathing and in-between the two, bath time for the local residents before they head out to work...

We double-back on ourselves and walk back towards where we started, and then continue beyond that until we reach the main burning ghat. This one looks a lot more formal; the wood neatly stacked at the top of the steps, right by the side of a massive sets of scales. Some Indian guy shows us to the viewing platform and explains a bit more about the process – who gets cremated here, how the type of wood shows your place in society, likewise the proximity to the river. It is all interesting stuff, but we know his hand will be held out for a tip within minutes... From the viewing platform we see body after body laid out on frames, like wooden stretchers. They are all covered in a shroud, awaiting their turn to be washed in the Ganges before being set alight in front of the male family members, and subsequently having their ashes taken away by the river. The funeral pyres along the ghats burn constantly, day and night - you can only look on at a respectful distance with awe, for the deceased and their family this is what they have always wanted.

After some banana pancakes at Spicey Bites we carry on walking along the steps by the river, there are a lot of people about, sunset boat trips are what they are all selling and we negotiate a price for an hour trip later in the day. Weddings are also extremely popular here; we have seen at least five already – part of their ritual also involves a blessing from the Ganges. They do seem to like a decorated horse for the wedding, they can be hired just like we would a limousine. We never see anyone on the horse so not sure what part they play on the big day...

The sunset boat cruise is good, the towering buildings of the ghats in a range of styles slowly obscure the setting sun, leaving a reddish glow behind them. It is also the most auspicious time to be cremated, the Manikarnika Ghat has at least twelve pyres alight as we sail past at a respectable distance, the whole steps are just covered in patches of orange flames and shrouded in black smoke. The young rower who took us out was a great guide, pointing out various sights and telling us about the meaning of the Aaarti ceremony on the Dashashwamedh ghat that we are going to see next. Aarti is a ritual displaying devotion by using fire as an offering. The recipient of the offering is the Goddess Ganga, affectionately sometimes referred to as Ma Ganga, the goddess of the holiest river in India. The Aarti takes place every sunset near the Kashi Vishwanath Temple without fail. We had seen them washing the plates and fancy lamps in the river this afternoon, not really knowing what they were, perhaps they were table adornments from a local restaurant had gone through our heads! They do look a bit like those fancy cake stands that your Nan may have had...

To a backdrop of drumming the devotees draped in saffron coloured robes spread out the plates and lamps before them. The blowing of a conch shell signals the start and the wafting of incense and the circling of the large flaming lamps begins. It is a noisy affair, but the sandalwood from the sticks is pleasant, they are the ones that we always take home! We stay and watch for half hour; in all honesty we are not the most spiritual of people, and it is very repetitive – but at least we can say that we witnessed it. It is amazing just how many people have hired boats to view the ceremony from the water rather than the wooden benches, never seen so many rowing boats at one time, hundreds of them! While the crowds are still watching the Aarti, we head off back to Spicey Bites - vegetarians for the night as we order a chilli paneer and a cashew nut curry. What a day, and to round it off perfectly we find our way back to the Baba guesthouse without getting lost at all...

A new day and we had slept well, or at least until we were awoken by the sounds of monkeys running by our window, and across the tin roofs below, not an everyday experience! After a leisurely breakfast, same place as yesterday, we make the short journey through the narrow alleyways and onto the ghats. Our destination is the Assi Ghat, the southernmost one within the city, but also one of the largest, extremely popular with tourists, due to its proximity to the Monkey Temple. The walk is beyond where we ventured too yesterday, so on route we pass the bathers, buffaloes and bodies awaiting cremation on the Harishchandra ghat.

It is only our second day here in Varanasi and as silly as it may seem, the shock of seeing the bodies, albeit covered in a shroud, no longer phases us – it is just what happens here, all day every day. This morning there seems to be more pyres lit and in the brief time it takes us to pass by, we see two more bodies being carried down the steps towards the river. It seems that locals make a living by accosting visitors and telling them about what they are seeing, this ghat will take the deceased of any religion apart from Islam... that is all we learnt as we continued our walk making our excuses before he could ask for his tip! Assi ghat is a hive of activity; more boat trips for sale, snake charmers, ice-cream sellers, tuk-tuk drivers and cycle-rickshaws all wanting to take you somewhere... We watch a snake charmer for a short while before heading up the steps and going off in search of the Durghar Temple, often referred to as the Monkey Temple due to the sheer number of them wandering around it! We ask directions, more than once, but are getting nowhere, the advice we are given often contradicts what the last person said! With cycle-rickshaws in plentiful supply we hail one down and ask for a price, it seems reasonable to us so we jump aboard.

What follows is a lot longer journey than what we were expecting, the guidebook describes it as minutes away from Assi ghat (hence why we were planning on walking), but at least it is not us doing the pedalling... When we finally reach our destination, we are dropped off at the Sankat Mochan Hanuman Temple, our driver points across at it, saying monkey, monkey. The penny drops with us, Hanuman is the Hindu monkey god, or at least depicted in that way, so where we wanted to go to was lost in translation! Now we are here we take a quick look around, before promptly getting a tuk-tuk to the correct one. One thing we have learned from this episode is that these Indian cycle-rickshaw wallahs work extremely hard for their money!

Durghar Temple is not the most attractive one we have ever seen; it is painted a deep brick red for starters! We discover more about it, of its importance to the Hinduism religion and how the story goes that the icon of Durga was not made by man but just emerged on its own... Constructed in the eighteenth century it was dedicated to the Goddess Durga, the pond by the side was once connected to the river Ganges. The red 'paint' is more relevant when it is explained that it is representative of the deity Durga, and it is not Dulux, but an ochre, a naturally produced red pigment. The monkeys are here in abundance, as are the signs warning you about them! The noises alone keep you on your toes, grip onto your hat and keep your bag fastened tight! It has been a good morning, two temples visited and while neither are in the must-see architecturally category, they have been interesting. We find our way back to the ghats in minutes, a herd of buffalos guiding us as they make their way down for a daily bath and scrub.

At the top of the steps a few ghats along we sit and enjoy a cup of chai at the Everest Café and have a bird's eye view looking down on all the action below. Slightly to our right are the buffalos, directly in front some laundry activity going on and a little further to the left we can see smoke coming from the funeral pyres. I am ninety-nine percent certain that the smell of that laundry will not be recreated as a fabric conditioner fragrance any time soon! Our afternoon is spent exploring the narrow lanes close to our digs, the night we arrived we never believed we would have got this brave! What we soon realised is that if you can find your way down to the river, making our way back to the Baba Guesthouse is easy. Cows are the biggest problems in these alleys, while locals just give them a shove, we are still a bit timid, almost apologising to the cow and hoping we soon reach a wider part where we can pass. Monkeys are also an issue, jumping from building to building, but also crapping from a great height; we originally thought we had a close encounter, dodged a bullet if you like, but soon realise that Alison is modelling the latest in monkey poo on the sleeve of her T-shirt.

As we make the short distance back home the drums of a wedding party are getting louder and louder, we even see the wedding horse, all decorated up and covered in intricate rugs (throws?), but unfortunately no sign of the wedding party. They must be in a courtyard somewhere within the labyrinth of passageways around here, we were interested in seeing what was going on. By night we do not wander too far, having seen the Aarti ceremony the previous night we just head out for some food at the Baba restaurant. Once again quite happy to be vegetarians for the night, we cannot believe that meat free options back home are this tasty. It is a bonus that the Wi-Fi is excellent, so we have a catch up with family and then head back to our room to kill bugs and relax.

Not such a good night's sleep, in fact it was quite restless. We were disturbed by a combination of insects and mosquitoes in the room and a change of bedding arrangement in the middle of the night. We swap the sheet from the mattress around with our furry overthrow and sleep much better. It was at this point that we cancelled the impending alarm set to wake us up in time for the sunrise, that can wait until tomorrow. Breakfast is a leisurely affair at the Baba restaurant, we have ticked the boxes of everything that we wanted to do here in Varanasi, today can be an unrushed wander along the ghats, down the alleys and passages, who knows what we will discover?

This morning appears to be the day of the stoned Babas; our idea of a Baba is a holy man, living a devout and basic life, even reclusive, these guys look the part - saffron coloured robes, long beards etc. That is where the similarities end, the ones we see were either stoned, asking for cigarettes, or charging people to have their photographs taken; and with not being smokers we were happy to pay the twenty rupees for a snap! Perhaps some of them are into the spirituality of the place but many are there for the photo opportunities and the 'guru Dakshina,' money to me and you! To be fair it is great to see them about, they add colour, mystery and another dimension to the place – and just because they are no longer matching our pre-conceived idea, does it really matter...

We carry on walking, looking to find our way beyond the Manikarnika ghat, the main burning place. Because of the nature of the place, you cannot just walk through it, yet the ghats by the river go way past this point, if we can find our way through the passages and streets beyond. We give it our best shot, more cows and dogs, even goats, but it is also the main route to bring the bodies through and down to the river. We know we need to head away from the river, take a right turn and then double back further on, but we only find dead ends... in the end we admit defeat. With nothing much to do we take a coffee break before heading back towards the Harishchandra ghat, a body is just being taken down to the river for the ritual bathing. Curiosity gets the better of us, so we take a seat on a step a good distance away and watch the entire process.

The body is brought back up from the river and placed on an unlit pyre, the head is further blessed with water from the river and the mourners walk around the body, a good number of times. The pyre is lit and the flames soon flare up and consume the body; before long, the feet that were pointing upwards in the twelve o' clock position have flopped right round to the five and seven on the clock. The melting fat and sinew feeds the flames, at speed too. One of the workers from the ghat folds back in an arm that has dropped down to one side, poking it back into the trunk area. The feet eventually drop off and the ghat worker folds the rest of the legs into the chest, guess the skin, ligaments and muscles have all now gone so the body can be moved at his will. It is surprising just how quick the entire process is, from shrouded body to a folded pile of bones in around an hour; we are told that it takes a further four hours for the bones to be ash and then the staff from the ghat just sweep the ash remains of the flesh and bones into the river. That is the same river that people are using for their daily ablutions, their laundry; there is little wonder why the river Ganges is one of the most polluted bodies of water in the world.

At the Everest Café we talk about what we have just seen, neither of us found it gruesome. It is far more graphic than what we do with our deceased back home, but it still has the same sense of ritual that we put into our services. Life, and death, in many parts of India really do happen in full view of everyone, it is just a completely unique way of life to what we take for granted. The buffaloes return for their evening bathe...

The alarm wakes us from what has been a better night's sleep. It might be early but there are lots of people about, and plenty of monkeys too... The sunrise has been worth getting up for, and the river has a lovely glow shining on it. The boat trips have already started, is there no time of day when they are not running? For us it is just a case of taking a few photos before returning to our room and packing our bags. By seven we are checking out of the Baba Guesthouse, the man from reception leads us through the network of passageways; past the cows and their deposits plus a pair of dead rats. We soon reach the main road where Babaloo, the same guy who brought us here, is waiting for us. Goodbyes and our thanks are passed on before we head to the airport, hopefully missing the morning rush hour.

It is a smooth departure from Varanasi airport; no delays and no baggage to check in for us, time to sit down and enjoy our biscuits. On our transfer at Hyderabad airport security must be bored, they make us switch on all our battery-operated items and check that all our plugs do provide power... It is a first for us, but better to be on the safe side rather than the security be lax. By this point we are hungry and there is a KFC in the departure halls, so that will do nicely for lunch; we also manage to 'obtain' a good supply of chilli sauce sachets for our egg butties, we had been running low! There is a small delay before we get to board, but with a troupe of clowns wandering around the airport performing magic tricks for both children and adults that extra waiting time whizzes by. Once sat on the plane there is a further hold up, while a 'technical issue' is sorted, maybe an elastic band problem as we are back on a propeller driven plane again? Hopefully nothing too serious... With that 'issue' resolved it is time to fasten our seatbelts, take off and head up into the skies for our return to Goa.

Our trip is reaching it is close, we have seen everywhere and everything that we intended to, no mishaps or disasters – all that is left is for us to enjoy the beach and sun for the next ten days. Feelings are mixed; in some ways we are ready for home, seeing family and friends again, but on the other hand we had put so much time and effort into planning this adventure that it is sad that it is nearly over. Maybe it is with having been away for a few days that we notice how much hotter and humid it has become. Following a morning trip to the market and an afternoon cooking; the ceiling fan in the kitchen swirling around stifling air, the decision is made, no more cooking.

Days on the beach are now just stifling, the breeze of January and February seems to have disappeared, dipping in the sea to cool off is not so pleasant either – tiny little jellyfish in places, nothing too painful but you can definitely feel them! Lunches of salad and chips are still good though and a Rovers Return Sunday roast was once again a reminder of home. Despite the beach vendors pestering us daily we still have not bought a selfie-stick!

We spend a great afternoon in Madhu's, by chance we get chatting with a lovely Indian couple, Wishy and Meena from Haryana, close to Delhi. Wishy speaks perfect English, it sounds like he is very well travelled, Meena is a little shy, but her language skills are also good. As the conservation flows it appears that they were friends of Steve Irwin, the deceased Australian zookeeper / environmentalist – his family is visiting them for an annual celebration in September, a trip they make every year. They give us a cashew fruit to try, it is like an apple, only smaller; a strange taste, almost sweet initially but a sour after effect. It sounds like they have been 'scrumped' from an old childhood stomping ground! We were only planning to stay for a couple of drinks but they insist upon more drinks and crisps, their treat; it sounds like they do not usually drink at all but are enjoying the freedom that Goa offers! It turns into the full afternoon and before saying goodbyes we exchange email addresses; they look a little wobbly as they set off walking back to their hotel...

It has got to the stage where we are having to choose carefully on where we eat each night, with only a handful of meals left we need to plan what dish where, would hate to run out of evenings and miss out on a favourite! Drinking at night is always at Madhu's, by now we are never alone as we have become friends with so many other couples, although some of them are beginning to leave for home (many have been here since November). Goodbyes are said to Mike and Sylvia, a fantastic down to earth Yorkshire couple who enjoy our love of Whitby. Ken and Mo are still here, though they have had an eventful time – Mo has been fitted with a stent after having a heart attack on the beach while we were away in Varanasi. Amazingly she was in and out of hospital in a matter of days and carrying on her holiday as if nothing happened within the week. Ken and Mo surprise us, they say they have been coming to Goa for the last twenty years but are tired of the place! Mo says that Ken has said that before, then the thought of winter strikes... he says he is adamant this time. Chef is a permanent fixture, supplying us with pate that is suitable for any meal – we have eaten it late at night, for breakfast and for a mid-afternoon snack!

The day before we depart our morning is spent giving the apartment a very thorough clean, final bits of washing done and then a last trip to the market to purchase gifts for Valerie, Savio and Sovann. The treat for Valerie is a little strange, she loves bananas... the chocolate is for Savio and Sovann, we think they are addicted to the stuff, plus a big cake from a local bakery. We get to sample the cake ourselves later as Savio knocks on our door and insists that we come to the shop for the slicing ceremony!

The final night in Madhu's and its goodbyes all around. We will miss Chef - he is entertaining in different ways at different times. By afternoon he is great company, incredibly wise and thought provoking, full of stories from his early years growing up in Mumbai. By night he can rub some people up the wrong way, often blunt, a cutting sense of humour, but always amusing – we will miss his 'Yabba-Dabba-Do,' Fred Flintstone impressions whenever a particularly attractive young Russian lady walks by!

Packing our bags for the final time does not take long. It is a strange morning, lots of clock watching – just killing time until our 11:15 a.m. pick up. The keys for the apartment are handed back to Valerie, and fortunately she had called Mr Diego earlier to confirm our collection time as he had forgotten all about us! More goodbyes and then the short journey to the airport. Oman Air, via a one-night stay in Muscat (at their expense), is all that remains of our trip. Every other time we have left Goa it has been on a flight departing in the early hours of the morning, and always been chaotic – today is so much more relaxed, we are soon checked in and with our baggage offloaded there's just immigration left to navigate.

It is the same journey as we made two years ago, a Qatar Airways flight from Heathrow to Goa, via Doha. Unfortunately, it is just the two weeks holiday again this time – a week or so earlier Alison secured a new job, and I have an interview lined up for when we return. Unusually we have nothing planned to do once we reach Goa, this will test our ability to relax and unwind to the limit. Our first hiccup is on the mini-bus from the airport car park to the terminal, Alison suddenly remembers that she hasn't put her clothes in the case that she had ironed and hung up in the spare room. Now, to me that sounds like a deliberate act, seeing a sneaky opportunity to spend money on new clothes whilst we are away.

For anyone who visited India in November 2016, they may well remember that money was a problem, they were in the process of changing their notes. Many repeat visitors were caught with currency that either was no longer usable, many others were forced to queue daily at the ATM, if you could find one open, to withdraw a solitary two thousand rupee note. Forewarned, we had been able to pay for our accommodation, sending the money to Mr. Wilfred by bank transfer beforehand, so that avoided one problem – but the rest of the holiday we remember the money situation being a pain. A fresh newly printed big denomination note that everyone was reluctant to take, they had no change....

Our funniest moment of the whole holiday was on our arrival at the Casa Aleixo. With it being our second visit and knowing where the staff slept, we were to wake them up when we arrived, and they would then let us into our room. That all sounds simple, what had not been considered was how spending your afternoon off drinking, makes you almost impossible to wake up! The driver had dropped us off by the gate and we had taken our luggage as far as the door before heading down the garden to where Mr. Wilfred's staff slept, I started with a gentle tap on the door. No sign or sound of any movement, so I knock a little louder – still nothing. My next level of knock hurt my knuckles; I could knock no harder than that, and I was worried that lights in the house would come on, me having woken everyone. I try the door, its unlocked and there is a shape of a body lying in the bed. It is like a mummified body, no doubt he is wrapped himself head to toe in the sheet to avoid mosquitos, so I give him a little shake. Nothing. It had even crossed my mind by this stage that he was dead! My shaking gets a little more vigorous, until the stage where I have both hands on his chest, bouncing him up and down in his bed – if he was dead, I was practically performing heart massage on him. With a jump, he woke... much to our relief.

Next morning, we had our breakfast in the same room as before and just as we were about to leave Mr. Wilfred came in, apologising for our problem in getting in last night. We were not even going to mention it, not wanting to get the lad into any trouble, but it sounds like his young member of staff had spilled the beans himself, even confessing that a beer or two was responsible for his deep sleep. With the secret out I told him the whole story, we all had a right good laugh about it, including young Mr. Sleepyhead who by now was back collecting the empty plates. A lazy morning around the pool provides us with a chance to snooze and make up for lost sleep from our journey.

We had a little bit of money to start our holiday, but nothing like enough to see us through the fortnight. The search for an ATM was on; no queue meant no money, it was empty. It was an ATM with a lengthy queue that we were after. This was to be an almost daily occurrence, when it was your turn to withdraw, the maximum you could take out was two thousand rupees, issued in a single note. Luckily, we had a bank card each so we could make two withdrawals each day. Two thousand rupees is twenty pounds sterling, so not a huge amount, but that goes quite a way here. The problem does not end there though... no one has a lot of change, so trying to use that note is more difficult than you can imagine. Paying for an evening meal with a couple of drinks might be fine, settling a bill for a pair of drinks – awkward!

Of course, Alison needed some clothes, her clever ploy or forgetfulness means she has minimal items with her. That is where we get our first two thousand note changed, a deliberately calculated spend of twelve hundred rupees would leave both the stall holder happy and us with some smaller notes. The whole holiday continued along this theme; a wander round to find a loaded ATM, wait for anything between thirty minutes to an hour for your turn, enter your PIN and take your solitary note. Evening meals were the best opportunity to cash it, they were usually our biggest spend of the day. Even on a day when you had enough cash to see you through, it still played on your mind – what if all the ATM's in Calangute were empty tomorrow? Will they be refilled over the weekend? If Mike and Sylvia are in Madhu's tonight, we can take turns at settling both bar tabs, that would make life easier for us both. In some ways it was a comical situation, in others a blight on the holiday. Rather than heading to the beach or lazing around the pool we must have lost ten or more hours queuing.

Our first evening meal was at our favourite place from last year, Kindmans. It stands a little back off the main Calangute to Baga road, the final fifty metres or so are up a rough track, but well enough lit to avoid the sleeping dogs. It is a Ken hot Vindaloo, as good and as hot as earlier in the year and although I feel slightly disloyal, it was better than what we had eaten at Mirabai's earlier today. When it comes to paying, we are given credit, our bill was around the thousand-rupee mark but Peter says if you are coming back within a few days settle your account then. Reading between the lines, he has no change – or minimal, so doing all he can to hang onto it for as long as he can. That is no problem by us, of course we are going back, at least twice more... Madhu's was busy, but no sign of anyone we knew. Ken and Mo said that they were giving Goa a miss, but we took that with a pinch of salt. Mike and Sylvia were not about either, maybe it was a market night and they had gone there instead? We would no doubt have drunk a little too much, that first night's exuberance has been to blame for many a hangover, or at least a delicate start to the next morning.

Valerie was her usual self, smiling and as enthusiastic as ever. Even though a lot of her business is based upon money exchange she was in the same boat, she had none either! It was good to chat, but her office may as well have had revolving doors – every other minute someone would pop their head through, looking for currency exchange. Sovann is growing up fast, but still loves chocolate that we were able to bring again on this visit. All being well we will go out for a meal sometime together, an evening out that we always look forward to and have really enjoyed on our previous visits.

As we walk to the beach, we carry on the routine that we developed earlier in the year. A big bottle of water from the little stall on the roundabout by Redondo's before continuing down Beach Road. Shoes off at the bottom of the steps and then paddle our way, ankle height through the sea until we reach the Rovers Return. Nothing has changed, the same yellow sunbeds and lots of faces that we recognise from previous years. A combination of reading and splashing around in the sea to cool off sees us through the day, or at least late enough to allow the purchase of samosas on the way home. We give the Red Lion a miss, it has not been the same since Frankie left – he has his own scooter business these days, we often bumped into him earlier in the year by the market, life was on the up for him.

There is still no sign in Madhu's of Mike and Sylvia, from their previous years routine that is unusual. By no means were they in every night, but it was rare for them to be missing two nights running. We know they were planning on being in Goa as they rent the same apartment each year, leaving some of their belongings locked away here. Maybe tomorrow? It is not the same without the Chef being sat at his usual table either. Everything else was the same though, the beer was cold, the Honey Bee and Old Monk was as good as usual and even the ice bucket had been upgraded. One of these times we will find it has been converted into a cocktail bar, where would we drink then?

Within four or five days we were bored, or at least not enjoying it as much as you should a holiday. Maybe it was too soon after our last visit, we had spent two months here earlier in the year and everything seemed the same, only this time we had no purpose. We had enjoyed having the apartment, we liked going to the market and even enjoyed all the cooking. Making our own breakfasts and watching MasterChef Asia meant it was gone ten a.m. before we were out and about, the days took less filling and were broken up more. Our only essential task this visit was to withdraw money, and that was just the proverbial pain in the neck. Even the evenings were not so much fun, there was still no sign of our friends, and although we happily chat to other people it is just not the same. We ask about Chef, how is he getting on and does he ever get out for a drink anymore?

We had been latecomers to Facebook, neither of us had joined until being made redundant last year – it would be a good way to stay connected with a lot of old friends and work colleagues. It also meant that we had been keeping up with the goings on with Chef, a Madhu's stalwart. When we had been here earlier this year, he was walking with a frame having had a hip replacement, sadly his health had taken a turn for the worse. Gangrene in his good leg had initially started in his toes, an operation removing them to prevent it spreading further had been unsuccessful. By August he was facing an amputation above the knee, and although the operation had gone well there is no such thing as social care in India. Even on one leg he was having to make a living, baking pies for local restaurants and dabbling in other businesses, even letting apartments – anything that would help keep the roof over his head and pay for his caretaker. Today we have some books to drop into him, and a birthday bottle of whisky, albeit a day or two too late.

With instructions of where he is living, we make the short journey on foot, crossing over the main road and taking a left past Toff Toffs, heading in the direction of our very first visit and the Aldeio Bello. His door is open, and as we knock, he sees us and invites us in. He looks well in the face, but has difficulty propping himself up, or at least adjusting himself into a more upright position. It is good to see him, his determination has to be admired but the sad reality is he has no choice, there is no safety net to fall back on like we have at home. In many ways he is his usual self; chatty, witty, good company. His caretaker slices us a piece of birthday cake, one from the bakery, not a Chef special with a little bit of his magic ingredient added... After about an hour we leave, he is grateful for the books and whisky and we wish him well in his onward recovery and burgeoning business interests. Sadly, that was the last we were ever to see of him.

Having gone into detail of everywhere else we have visited on our travels around India, a bit more about Goa... A brief history lesson immediately explains why Goa is so different from the rest of India; from 1510 Goa was under Portuguese colonial rule, and that would last for four and a half centuries, right through until 1961. The influence of Portugal on Goa meant that Christianity was the main religion and way of life, and whilst the culture remains an amalgamation of east meets west, it is those years of western rule that still holds sway. The religious influence is perhaps the biggest single factor that differentiates Goa from the rest of the country, much of what attracts tourists to Goa would not be acceptable in most parts of the country – laying on beaches in trunks and bikinis does not fit in with Hindu (or Muslim) ideals.

Goa is the smallest state in India, but also one of the wealthiest – much of that brought in by visiting tourists, although away from the coast it is rich in minerals and ores. Agriculture is shrinking in importance but it remains a big player in coconut cultivation. Why does it attract so many western tourists – let's face it from November to March the weather is constant sunshine, how many places can guarantee that? The people, so friendly and welcoming are key ingredients and with barely a culture change it provides most of what you could do in say the Canary Islands. For many the food plays a big part and let us not gloss over the cheap nights out. Goa is famous for its low-priced beer, wine and locally produced spirits due to its very low excise duty on alcohol. Have you noticed that your bottle always says for sale in the state of Goa? For better or worse, in 1976 it also became the first state in India to legalize some types of gambling, so presumably playing bingo before then would quite rightly have been a criminal offence...

We have only visited North Goa but enjoy walking along the long sandy beaches, yet it would be difficult to call it a paradise. Sadly, it is not very clean, many visitors lovingly refer to Goa as 'Paradise in a Dustbin,' and it is hard to disagree. Maybe the next generation will make a difference, the guys we met on the train journey from Hampi appreciated that it is a big issue that does need resolving. Calangute itself is part of the three small resorts that make up the hive of activity of the Candolim – Calangute – Baga tourist mecca, or the CCB belt. If you are feeling energetic you can walk between them all, along the beach or the road that links them together. Candolim is the quieter of the three, Baga is the liveliest, attracting young domestic tourists; if you fancy a late night, (early hours of the morning), clubbing or mixing with the local youngsters, this is where it is at. Calangute nestles between the two, the happy medium and gives you the option of eating and drinking, or catching up with friends in any of them. Demographic wise, the visitors from the UK tend to be mature, (ok older), although we have noticed that even during our eight years visiting that the average age must be coming down. Our first visit took us by surprise, lots of older people with fantastic tans and shiny white teeth, all having a wonderful time!

If we were to have one complaint it is that perhaps it panders too much to the UK tourist, and in doing so it neglects its own charm. Cambodia and Vietnam have both had a huge surge in visitor numbers but have kept their own traditional way of doing things. It is the old adage, do you travel to discover new experiences, to explore and to be taken out of your comfort zone, or do you want a break in warm weather and home comforts, familiarity? There is no wrong answer, and often the two crossover – while we would never order a Domino's pizza or pop into McDonalds for a burger it is only right that the locals have that option. Up until staying for those two months earlier this year we had always turned our nose up at the Sunday lunch options, but not anymore - you can get a fantastic Sunday lunch, roast beef, Yorkshire pud, the works... we had missed a taste of home.

The remainder of our holiday passed; Mr. Wilfred and his wife prepared us a lovely lunch the day before we left – two fish dishes, there would have been a third if it had not got dropped on being removed from the oven! They are a lovely couple, incredibly wise and have seen a lot of change in their time. Unfortunately, they do not see our hope that India will ever be litter free coming to fruition, the deep-rooted caste system means that many see sweeping up or cleaning of any kind as below them. Another of his gripes was tourists and their over generosity! Visitors who compare prices to back home, and then tip because it is so much cheaper; that is why he arranges transfers from the airport for his guests – a white face would pay double the going rate... and then tip on top of that! In his eyes this creates a problem for the locals, taxi and tuk-tuk drivers have become greedy or lazy – they would sooner play cards all day and rip three people off than do a solid day's work. Come the off-season and locals will not or cannot afford to pay their inflated fares, the driver has made his money so you take it or leave it...

We tell him we have similar problems back home, but with houses; families in tourist hotspots, are often driven away from where they have grown up, displaced and unable to afford a home due to holiday lets or second home-owners pushing prices up to unaffordable levels. It is quite a depressing conversation, and we remember back to a few months ago where Valerie would buy our prawns and then we would reimburse her, she knew we would be charged a far higher price. The bread man story and the Post Office incident make Mr. Wilfred smile... the locals see us as wealthy, and fair game to exploit. Today's conversation echo what the Chef has told us in the past, watch the locals he would always say, be that at the market or in a restaurant – see what they get charged, do they leave tips. By the end of the afternoon we have enjoyed a few beers, and put the world to rights, but still do not know exactly what Mr. Wilfred did (or does) for a living.

Mike and Sylvia never did appear in Madhu's, we missed our nightly chats – be that about Whitby weekend breaks or talking football or politics, always amicably as we share the same principles. I dropped Mike an email after a few days, but got no reply. On our return home we would do a little detective work, we knew where they lived so if we could find an address, we could drop a letter their way. For the first time ever, we were ready for going home, and unusually for us not certain when we would next return. We concluded that wherever we had gone for a two-week break would have felt a little flat, the months of planning following redundancy last year and that four months plus away would take some living up to. We need somewhere new to explore, Goa is that tried and tested well-worn comfortable pair of slippers – it is time to venture to horizons new.

Back home I found the address for Mike and Sylvia, courtesy of phone directories and websites. Sylvia replied to our letter with desperately sad news. In the summer of 2015 Mike had been diagnosed with an inoperable brain tumour, and was to pass away just before the New Year. Rest in peace Mike, a lovely warm-hearted guy, great company and taken far too early. We keep in touch with Sylvia, and try to visit whenever we are passing her way – she is doing brilliantly, has great neighbours and friends where she lives and spends a lot of time with their daughters and grandchildren.

By February 2016 Chefs landlord wanted him out of his apartment, the rent was being paid but he was still being forced into searching for alternative accommodation. Facilities, or rights for people with disabilities do not extend to India and a home for aged men looked like his only option. Through Facebook a crowdfunding campaign was set up to raise money for a wheelchair, to help him be more self-dependant be that in a home, but hopefully in his own apartment. All of this was played out on social media, in the end his landlord set a deadline, he did not want the trouble of a disabled tenant. Help was on the way from his many friends, but the Chef was a proud yet stubborn man. Tragically he took his own life after enjoying one final night of backgammon, whiskey and no doubt a few spliffs - RIP Chef. From this terrible situation came some good, the funds that had been coming in to help Chef were used to purchase wheelchairs for other needy people, some went into old folks' homes and one to a school for the disabled, all gifted in his memory.

Winter 2021 - Goa (Cancelled due to Covid)

After what seems like an age, we were planning to return to Goa in winter 2021 for the first time since November 2016. I think we knew when we left that year it would be a while before we returned, but never suspected it would be this long! We were both in new jobs by Christmas 2016, but still managed trips to South Africa, Sri Lanka and Nepal in the two years that we were working, so we can hardly complain. South Africa was truly amazing, Cape Town the wine regions and then Kruger National Park for a few days' safari. Both Sri Lanka and Nepal have vibes of India, so maybe getting that 'fix' prolonged our sabbatical. However, neither of us really liked our jobs... so by December 2018 we had both handed in our notices – the travelling bug had got us well and truly.

A flight to Bangkok in January 2019, before onward travels took us first into and around Cambodia for a month before heading to Vietnam for a further three. Every mile was covered on terra firma, all on buses apart from a single train journey – what an adventure. Avoiding cold English winters was the plan; January 2020 was Malaysia and Borneo, before having to return home earlier than planned, like many others, due to the Covid situation. We loved our visit to Malaysia, excellent value hotels and hostels with tasty street food stalls, evening meals never cost us more than two pound each. There is a big Indian influence on Malay dishes anyway, but if that wasn't enough each town or city we visited had its own 'Indian Quarter' where we could satisfy our cravings.

Come January 2021 we had been hoped to tag a month in Goa onto our travels, but the Covid pandemic put paid to that. The current visa situation continues to put us off returning – fingers crossed the E-visa is back available sooner rather than later. Our decision is based on the cost as much as the inconvenience of having to attend for an appointment, I guess depending on where you live affects the nuisance value and additional expense of that in-person visit? The price of those visas, plus travel to the consular office etc, would pay for a whole month's accommodation in much of South East Asia for the two of us!

We will be back at the first opportunity; Shimla is next on our list and then who knows where next...

Final Thoughts

So that is the end, or at least for now. We can endorse India's advertising strapline, it truly is 'Incredible India!.' But where blew us away, did anywhere disappoint – would we really do it all over again?

Starting with the last question, that is the easy one to answer. We have loved every minute and all the different experiences along the way. In a heartbeat we would do it all over again, and probably appreciate it even more. There is so much more to take in, places that are so vast that you would still find something that you had missed the first time around. The stories behind the places add to the picture, and in writing this I have learned so much more than what I knew at the time. Our guides have always been superb and knowledgeable, so it is not a criticism of them, but in that moment when you are there, feasting your eyes on the sights it is difficult to take everything else in – so many dates, Mughals and maharajas.

In answer to where or what disappointed I would say nowhere, every single place had its merits, beauty or story, not everywhere or everything was as we imagined. Some things in life are hyped up so much that it is difficult, or even impossible that they will meet or surpass your expectations, be that a film, hotel or a restaurant. The reverse is also true, some of the places that we had never even heard of, or knew little about were amongst our favourites. Trying to compare different places is almost impossible too, its apples and pears – both are fruits but that is where the similarity ends. Having thought long and hard though we do have our favourite, our own 'Jewel in the Crown'...

We enjoyed the Taj Mahal, there is no doubt that we did not see it at its best due to the weather when we visited, but that is the luck of the draw. What a building though, truly magnificent, iconic is the only way to describe it. For us however it had that missing ingredient, it is hard to put our finger on it – perhaps it is because it is so instantly recognisable that it held no surprises, it was exactly what we expected. Maybe our first impression from that drive into Agra is to blame, the view from across the polluted river would not have helped either. Our lasting memory is one of a beautiful building, one of the new seven wonders of the world, but located in a city that we did not like at all. Even the great romantic anecdote is tainted once you dig deeper and learn more about Shah Jahan. The fairy-tale story is a cover, in reality he was power hungry and executed most of his rivals to the throne, including multiple members of his own family!

Varanasi... where do you start? It is more of a life experience than looking at a particular landmark, so difficult to categorise. We loved our time here, the ghats and activity on the Ganges must be seen to be believed, and even then, on occasions we took a second glance just to make sure. When we first arrived, we were unsure, even intimidated by the tiny passageways and cramped alleys - often with a cow blocking our path. The cremations were fascinating, not gory or shocking, but a quite different way of dealing with death to what we are used to. Life (and death), is played out in full view here, it is a complete assault on the senses and unique, unlike anywhere else we have ever visited.

Rajasthan, each city we have visited in that state has been brilliant; similar but also different at the same time, if that makes sense. We fell in love with Udaipur, such a relaxed place with that lake setting and the mountain backdrop. It was here that we finally found an Indian city that we were more than happy to navigate under our own steam. Jodhpur swiftly followed as that was the next stop on the same tour, the market under the shadows of that most brutal looking fort was timeless. If we were to visit Jaipur again, we would have no qualms about wandering around on our own, there was so much to admire in that compact city centre. Much more to explore than what we had time for unfortunately.

Hampi, if there was a prize for taking us by surprise it would be in the gold medal position. Until spending time in Goa we had never heard of it, no Michael Palin or Joanna Lumley documentaries, not even a minor 'celebrity.' It could be that our expectations were not as high as for some places, but by the time we left we were singing its praises. The history of the place, and how well so much of it has been preserved, the sheer size and the beautiful setting it sits in. Our only gripe is that one full day wandering around this impressive site is not long enough, somewhere that we will definitely return to.

Kerala we would happily revisit, we thoroughly enjoyed our tour but it was so close to the end of the season that many of the restaurants in resort were already shut. Our choice of accommodation would also be better if we were to go again, the Kovalum beach area rather than in one of the bays to the north. It would be good to visit in the height of season as it has such a mix of places to visit close by, an excursion to the nearby hill station of Munnar would be high on our list. The sea food was so good that we did not miss our nightly curry... we never did get a beer served out of a teapot though.

Of the other cities; Delhi is not somewhere that we ever warmed to. The permanent smog from the air pollution is unnerving, so we have never ventured far from our hotel alone. A fear of getting lost and not finding our way back due to the reduced visibility has hampered our independent exploring! We did enjoy our tour though; Qutb Minar and the Friday Mosque, Jama Masjid, will always be our first experiences of the scale and magnificence of Indian sites.

Mumbai, we need to do again. We only had twenty-four hours, and Alison was not feeling at her best either. What we see we loved, but there is so much more to do - experiences that we would love to take in - a Bollywood movie, or even a cricket match. A chance to explore the Gateway of India from closer quarters, and walk along Marine Drive as night falls are a few that spring to mind.

Mysore was pleasurable to explore on foot. Pedestrian friendly, wide-open boulevards, it felt a very cosmopolitan city. We had a relaxed time here, sauntering through the local markets as well as enjoying the grounds of the Palace. In reality though, we have seen the star of its show, and on a Sunday when it is illuminated, so unlikely to make a return visit.

Two places that deserve a special mention are Fatehpur Sikri and the Jain Temple at Ranakpur. They were both places that we dropped in at travelling between the headline acts! Fatehpur Sikri, on the outskirts of Agra was an abandoned city, yet it is so complete that it felt like being on a film set. There was something about it that we really enjoyed, the red sandstone buildings as intact as the day in which they were deserted.

We stopped at the Jain Temple at Ranakpur on our journey between Udaipur and Jodhpur. This place had the most impressive carvings that we have ever seen bar none. The craftsmanship that has gone into the white marble pillars, door frames and ceilings here is incredible, the detail is so crisp and precise that it could have been done yesterday. From the outside it is equally as stunning, and its place amongst the final seventy-seven contenders for the new wonders of the world in 2007 was well deserved. And we had never even heard of it...

For us the Golden Temple at Amritsar was our absolute favourite, it had the lot. The stories, the incredible beauty of the temple itself, the lake and the four intentionally different buildings around it, the langar, the welcome we received. It was truly magical, the serenity and the song, the fish in the lake, but all set in what is a working place. Most attractions, possibly every other one we have visited, had an entry fee, there income primarily is as a tourist attraction. Here it was different, it is a living, breathing place, a pilgrimage site and the world's largest canteen – tourists are just a by-product, but embraced into the whole experience and greeted with incredible hospitality. Throw in the joyous Wagah border experience and for us Amritsar and the Golden Temple was head and shoulders above everywhere else we visited.

That just leaves Goa. The place where all bar one of these adventures has begun. In a lot of ways, we cannot wait to return, yet on the other hand we also feel that our best experiences have passed. Nostalgia plays its part; nothing can beat discovering somewhere new for the first time, your first visit anywhere is usually the best. The second visit holds fewer surprises, not to mention the third, fourth... In some ways the familiarity is good, the holiday begins from day one – you already know your way around, where to eat, drink etc. That same familiarity also means that when you look back, you miss not only some of the old places but more importantly faces from the past – and that is the hard part.

We have had some of our best holidays starting from there and met some amazing people along the way who we now call friends. The Goans are kind, welcoming hosts – that is one of the things that we really miss, so for us it is just a matter of time before we get back. The Covid outbreak foiled our original intention for winter 2021, the current visa situation has put us off this year... so perhaps another attempt for winter 2023/24?

Valerie Travels

Valerie of Valerie Travels has been organising travel related tours and trips since the year 2000. We have personally been using her services since 2011, and have been so well looked after that we are more than happy to sing her praises.

Her website can be found at https://www.valerietravelsgoa.com/ and from there you can browse all the trips that she offers.

Excursions offered vary to suit all pockets - and how long you want to be away from the beach for! Staying within Goa there are overnight stays on a traditional rice boat or a bungalow with a waterfall view at the idyllic Wildernest Nature Resort. Travelling further afield there is of course the Golden Triangle, your ideal opportunity to see the Taj Mahal. Plenty of the trips that we have enjoyed are also listed there, Amritsar, Hampi, Mumbai, Varanasi, Kerala and Rajasthan. Some of these trips are four nights, five days away and are very flexible... one that has caught our eye is for Shimla, which can be tagged onto various other options in the north of the country. Maybe that is our next one to do?

When the world went into lockdown with the Covid pandemic Valerie turned her hand to another great love of hers, one that we were fortunate enough to have lessons in from her back in 2016... cookery. We can vouch that she is a fantastic chef and in a short time she gave us plenty of tips that have improved our Indian cooking no end. For anyone interested in enhancing their skills, or even considering cooking Indian dishes for the first time then take a look at her YouTube channel, the link is below.

https://www.youtube.com/@valsquicktipsandtricks

Also in this series ...

Backpacking: Not Just For The Young! Thailand : Cambodia : Vietnam : India

We have both always had a love of travel and over the years have got more adventurous in arranging it ourselves. What started as city breaks around Europe became excursions to parts of India whilst on holiday in Goa. One evening we had friends around who had returned from Vietnam and arranged the whole trip themselves, from then on we knew that was what we wanted to do whenever possible – so much more fun than browsing a brochure from the travel agents and following someone else's plan.

We soon discovered that we enjoyed budget travel and the people you meet are of like mind, pretty care free and chatty but full of information, tips and ideas. Why should budget travel and backpacking be the sole preserve of the young! We are by no means old, Alison a smidgeon over 50, Wayne a little under but both of the age where we need the toilet in the middle of the night!

OPPORTUNITY ARRIVES...

30th July 2015 and our employers go into administration, we both work there so for the first time in our lives neither of us have jobs. With our daughter being 21 and both sets of parents in good health was this our moment?

Over a glass of wine it was something we had often talked about, always so envious of people who we had met during our two weeks break who were travelling for months. Financially it was possible – but did we have the nerve?

What follows is the story of our travel as we wander through Thailand, Cambodia, Vietnam and onto India.

Printed in Great Britain
by Amazon

25707787R00099